Marketing and Communication in Higher Education

In recent decades, higher education has seemingly witnessed a paradigmatic shift from government-controlled systems, in which higher education is for the public good, to a market-based system, in which higher education is a good for the public. Indeed, colleges, universities, and other institutions of higher education have adopted a kind of 'academic capitalism', wherein entrepreneurship, new product development, brand-building, aggressive promotion, and other marketing and communication activities are not only acceptable, but perhaps even necessary for institutional survival. The purpose of this series is to explore issues of marketing and communication in higher education. The series aims to be broad in scope, with individual volumes addressing a wide variety of issues in and around the marketing and communication in higher education... from student choice behaviours, to digital media tactics. The series embraces different disciplinary and methodological approaches, and features different national and cultural higher educational contexts. And the series publishes both solo-authored and edited volumes, which adopt descriptive, empirical, or critical perspectives.

Albert N. Greco

Scholarly Publishing in the Humanities, 2000–2024

Marketing and Communications Challenges and Opportunities

Albert N. Greco
Fordham University
Bergenfield, NJ, USA

ISSN 2946-4595   ISSN 2946-4609   (electronic)
Marketing and Communication in Higher Education
ISBN 978-3-031-66169-3   ISBN 978-3-031-66170-9   (eBook)
https://doi.org/10.1007/978-3-031-66170-9

Cover pattern © Melisa Hasan

This Palgrave Macmillan imprint is published by the registered company Springer Nature Switzerland AG.
The registered company address is: Gewerbestrasse 11, 6330 Cham, Switzerland

If disposing of this product, please recycle the paper.

Dedication For Elaine

ACKNOWLEDGMENTS

I want to thank Milana Vernikova, an excellent editor, for her interest and support for this book, and the superb staff at Palgrave Macmillan in the United States and abroad for their impressive assistance in the development and publication of this book.

I also want to acknowledge the impact a group of scholars had on my research and life, including historians Paul Mason, Steven Bela Vardy, and Samuel Astorino, and philosopher Aldo Tassi.

Disclaimer

A large number of trade publishing firms, university presses, commercial scholarly publishers, scholarly organizations and societies, and universities are mentioned and analyzed in this book. My wife and I do not own stock in any company. All of our financial assets are handled exclusively by TIAA, where I clearly have no say in buys and sells.

In addition, artificial intelligence (AI) was not utilized in the researching and/or writing of this book.

CONTENTS

LIST OF TABLES

Introduction to the Humanities and the Role of the Humanities in the History of Higher Education in the United States

Abstract The first printed book was published in Germany "about" 1450; it was *The Gutenberg Bible*. The first book printed and published in England was "about" 1475 by William Caxton; it was the first print edition of Geoffrey Chaucer's *The Canterbury Tales*. Oxford University Press (OUP) was the first university press (1478), and its first book was *Arch. G e. 8, Expositio in symbolorum apostolorum, Exposition of the Apostlic Creed*, by Rufinus of Aquilea. The first printed scholarly journal was the *Journal des Scavans*, launched in January 1665 in France. The first book printed in the American colonies was *The Bay Psalm Book* in 1640. In the American colonies, the majority of the earliest colleges were created to train individuals for the ministry, and the curriculum included the traditional academic fields in the humanities. Higher education in the United States grew slowly, but the humanities were the preeminent academic field until the new emphasis on science during World War II. After the war, the humanities sustained periods of growth and later concern about the "crisis in the humanities." This chapter investigates these issues and provides statistical data about the number of faculty and majors in the humanities.

Keywords Humanities • Academic fields • Higher education • Scholarly books • Scholarly journals • Academic libraries • Intellectual property • Gutenberg • Publishing history • Ted Levitt

A. N. Greco, *Scholarly Publishing in the Humanities, 2000–2024*, Marketing and Communication in Higher Education, https://doi.org/10.1007/978-3-031-66170-9_1

DEFINITIONS AND KEY TERMS

The *Merriam-Webster's Dictionary* defines "humanities" as "humanities plural: the branches of learning (such as philosophy, arts, or languages) that investigate human constructs and concerns as opposed to natural processes (as in physics or chemistry) and social relations (as in anthropology or economics)."[1]

In the United States, the humanities includes a broad number of academic fields and subjects including (in alphabetical order): African-American studies (literature, history, etc.); American studies (literature, history, etc.); art history; classical languages and literature (history, architecture, communications and publishing, English language and literature (including drama); filmed entertainment (motion pictures, television) and the performing arts; foreign language and literature (including drama); gender and women's studies (literature, history, etc.); history (various areas: America, Europe, Asia, etc.); linguistics; music history; philosophy (i.e., various schools of philosophy, including: "(1) all learning exclusive of technical precepts and practical arts; (2) the sciences and liberal arts exclusive of medicine, law, and theology, a doctor of philosophy; (3) the 4-year college course of a major seminary; and (4) religion and theology."[2]

While there will be references to many of these important academic categories, the emphasis will be on the following subject areas in the humanities: English language and literature, history, philosophy, and religion and theology.

In this book, the terms college, colleges, university, universities, and higher education will be used interchangeably. The terms scholarly book and scholarly books will be used interchangeably; publisher, publishers, publishing, and scholarly publishing will be used interchangeably; scholarly journal and scholarly journals will be used interchangeably; library, libraries, college library, college libraries, university library, university libraries, academic library, and academic libraries will be used interchangeably; society, societies, and learned societies will be used interchangeably; and museum, museums, and humanities museums will be used interchangeably.

THE KEY RESEARCH ISSUES, TOPICS, AND QUESTIONS INVESTIGATED IN THIS BOOK

Substantive issues and developments in the humanities are analyzed in this book, including the following. First, what significant events took place in society (e.g., the impact of Covid and the lockdowns; and inflation), higher education, digital technologies, and the humanities sectors between 2000 and 2024 that impacted colleges, academic libraries, the humanities, humanities societies, museums (with a humanities programs and exhibits), readers, and professors?

Second, what impact did these developments have on scholarly book and journal publishing in the humanities? Third, what impact did these developments have on professors and graduate students undertaking research in the humanities? Fourth, what impact did these developments have on intellectual property, "gender disparity," diversity, equity, and inclusion in the humanities and in publishing in the humanities? Fifth, what is the future of the humanities and humanities publishing and research in the United States?

Major topics that will be investigated include: (a) various publishing firms/operations that published scholarly books and scholarly journals in the humanities (i.e., university presses, commercial scholarly publishers, learned societies, trade book houses, libraries, city, county, state, and the U.S. government's humanities programs; and self-publishing firms); (b) the impact of innovative and disruptive technologies on scholarly publishing in the humanities; (c) changes in higher education funding, demographics, and society that impacted the humanities; (d) the importance of markets in the dissemination of new research in the humanities; (e) the impact of new effective, and at times ineffective, marketing, managerial, and financial theories and practices utilized by publishers in the humanities; (f) the impact and the development of open access (OA) guidelines, mandates, and regulations for scholarly books and scholarly journals; (g) the impact of dramatic changes in the sale and channels of distribution for scholarly books and journals; (h) the precarious situation of academic libraries, humanities societies, organizations, and museums (with a humanities collections/programs) regarding funding of their operations; (i) the impact of disintermediation (i.e., books sold online from a publisher's website directly to readers/consumers (D-2-C) rather than in the traditional channels of distribution; and (j) significant intellectual property, copyright infringement issues, rampant piracy, and the impact on publishers, authors, academic libraries, and readers.

However, in spite of the various challenges plaguing higher education and the humanities in the years between 1640 and 2000, major publishing houses remained in business (albeit because of mergers and acquisitions, which enabled some publishers to grow due specifically to acquisitions). Based on a detailed analysis of the humanities, and scholarly book and journal publishing in the humanities, the following theories or ideas will be examined and utilized in this book.

Some publishers evaluated recent business trends (e.g., the "4 Ps" in marketing: product, price, placement, and promotion in the humanities book and journal sectors) in order to understand and cope with the trends and uncertainty that marked the years after 2000. Unfortunately, some trends were unsettling (e.g., the ravages of piracy, the Covid lockdowns in 2020–2021, and the rapid and unparalleled emergence of artificial intelligence (AI) and ChatGPT in November 2022). A few publishers read the published business and economic literature on how the industry coped with the sudden impact of the Great Depression, World War II, and the "cold war." However, most of the relevant business research centered on the 12 major recessions as well as the massive technological innovations since 1948, and many publishers were not prepared for the massive Covid lockdowns, AI, or ChatGPT. So, relying on using the past to plan for the "Apocalypse" did not work effectively in the publishing industry. Other publishers relied on the major business and economic articles and books for guidance and a strategic game plan, including Ted Levitt's pivotal article "Marketing Myopia."[3]

To address these concerns, many publishing firms (but unfortunately not all of them) adopted an intriguing mix of marketing, management, economic, production (i.e., migrating from a traditional print product to a hybrid, both print and digital, and eventually to a only digital product). In addition, some publishers relied on the elusive quest for "scale" (i.e., economies of scale and mass production).

In essence, this book will analyze these trends. The book's goal is to understand why publishing scholarly books and journals in the humanities is, and will remain, a critically important yet complicated component of the higher education (and related areas) landscape.

Statistical Data

To analyze the important trends in the history of publishing humanities books and journals, substantive statistical data from a number of highly reliable databases were reviewed, including: *The Statistical Abstract of the U.S.*; the U.S. Department of Education (Education), National Center for Education Statistics (NCES); the U.S. Department of Commerce (Commerce), Bureau of the Census (Census); the U.S. Department of Labor (Labor), Bureau of Labor Statistics (BLS); the Association of

American Publishers (AAP); the Association of University Presses (AUP; formerly the Association of American University Presses, AAUP); the American Library Association (ALA); the Association of College Research Libraries (ACRL); the Modern Language Association (MLA); the National Endowment for the Humanities (NEH) and the NEH's Office of Federal/ State Partnership and the State and Jurisdictional Humanities Councils; the American Council of Learned Societies (ACLS); the American Academy of Arts & Sciences (AAAS); the Library of Congress (LC); *Publishers Weekly (PW)*; *The Library and Book Trade Almanac* (formerly *The Bowker Annual*); The National Endowment for the Arts (NEA); various humanities organizations (e.g., the American Historical Association (AHA)); etc.

HISTORICAL BACKGROUND

After centuries of individuals "printing" words and images using hammers and chisels on pieces of stone, later on pieces of wood, and then on the walls of caves, eventually scrolls were developed broadening somewhat access to readers. Later on authors created beautiful illuminated manuscripts that offered, at best, rather limited access to these manuscripts to readers because of literacy issues. Finally, in the fifteenth century, a mechanical system was devised to mass produce words and images printed on sheets of paper that were then bound into a portable book.

The first printed book was published in Germany "about" 1450 (i.e., maybe 1455) by Gutenberg; and it was *The Gutenberg Bible*. The first book printed in England was in 1475 (or possibly 1476) by William Caxton; and it was "the first ever print edition of Geoffrey Chaucer's *The Canterbury Tales*."[4] Oxford University Press (OUP) was the first university press (1478); and its first book was *Arch. G e. 8, Expositio in symbolorum apostolorum, Exposition of the Apostlic Creed*, by Rufinus of Aquilea.[5] Other major publishers emerged in Europe after the 1450s, including Brill (1683) and Macmillan (1843).

The first printed scholarly journal emerged two centuries after the printing of the *Gutenberg Bible*; and it was the *Journal des Scavans*, launched by Denis de Sallo in France in January 1665.[6] It was a rather eclectic journal, listing newly published books, obituaries, and important scientific experiments. While this journal was initially important in the history of scholarly journals, the decision by the Royal Society in England to create and launch their own journal, *Philosophical Transactions*, marked the beginning of the support from academic societies to assist scholars and scholarship.[7] While the name of this journal appeared to be a humanities publication, it was really a science, technology, and medical (STM) journal reflecting the seventeenth-century view of "philosophy." Eventually other societies in England, Europe, and the United States launched scholarly journals, including the American Philosophical Society, founded in 1743 by Benjamin Franklin, to promote useful knowledge.[8]

Clearly, the history of scholarly publishing in the humanities has had a rich history.

THE ROLE OF THE HUMANITIES IN THE HISTORY OF HIGHER EDUCATION IN THE UNITED STATES

Higher education institutions in Colonial America were modeled on the great medieval universities in England and Europe that emphasized the importance of the humanities (e.g., religion, philosophy, classical languages and literature, and history), including universities at Bologna (established in 1088), Paris (1150), Oxford (1167), Cambridge (1209), Padua (1222), Pisa (1343), etc.[9]

In the American colonies, the majority of the 19 earliest colleges were created originally under the auspices of a Protestant religious group to train individuals for the ministry (e.g., Harvard University was established in 1636 as a Puritan college). Some of the other early institutions of higher learning affiliated with a Protestant group included the College of William and Mary (1693), Yale (1701), Moravian (1742), Princeton (1746), Columbia (1754), and Rutgers (1766). However, several of the 19 colleges were non-sectarian, including Washington College (1723), Washington & Lee (1749), Pennsylvania (1755), and Pittsburgh (1770). The curriculum at many of these colonial colleges included the traditional academic fields in the humanities, including Latin, Greek, history, and philosophy.[10]

After the American Revolution and the creation of the United States, more colleges were created. Some of them were non-sectarian because of the outburst of democratic ideals after 1776; others had a religious orientation, including the launching of Protestant and Catholic colleges, but all of them emphasized the humanities.

Roger L. Geiger's historical work is a significant contribution to understanding the growth in the number of colleges, especially after 1820, a period he maintained represented a "renaissance" in the history of higher education in the United States. The years from the 1850s to the 1880s marked the beginning of what Geiger believed was the creation of modern higher education institutions with a curriculum that continued to emphasize the humanities but added electives and other academic disciplines.[11] However, very few individuals attended these early American colleges or universities because of tuition and related expenses. During those years, the U.S. population grew at first rather slowly after 1790 (when the first census took place the population was a small 3,929,214), but, between 1830 and 1860, the nation experienced an impressive increase in its population. The population stood at 31,443,322 in 1860 (+700.24% since 1790). Table 1.1 has the data.

Geiger described in some detail the important developments that transformed higher education from what had been an East Coast cluster of small humanities colleges to a more "national" form of higher education. The trends that transformed higher education in the United States included the following. First, the creation of the important land-grant colleges. The Morrill Act, passed during the Civil War on July 2, 1862, "made it possible for states to establish public colleges funded by the development or sale of associated Federal land grants."[12] This act opened the door to the practical arts in higher education to individuals in other regions of the nation. Second, the new primary emphasis on scholarly research, based

Table 1.1   U.S. population 1790–1860

Year	Total
1790	3,929,214
1800	5,308,483
1810	7,239,881
1820	9,638,453
1830	12,866,020
1840	17,069,453
1850	23,191,876
1860	31,443,322
1790–1860 Percent change	+700.24%

Source: *The Statistical Abstract of the United States 2024*; Table 1. N.B. All numbers rounded off

N.B. The various words, terms, and definitions used by various U.S. government departments and agencies were used "as is" in this book and in the various tables in the book

on the European orientation, was in the humanities. However, many areas of the social sciences and the sciences started to receive more research and funding, although the United States lagged behind the great science professors and facilities in Europe. Third, the creation of law and medical colleges helped round out the educational offerings in the United States.[13] Other scholars wrote about the development of colleges for women, including the important scholarship of Emily A. Langdom.[14] Some other scholars addressed and analyzed the exceptionally slow, but critically important, opening of colleges for African Americans; some of the superb studies that investigated this history included the important work of Marybeth Gasman[15] as well as the superb research of Robert Bruce Slater.[16]

Claudia Goldin and Lawrence F. Katz analyzed higher education between the years 1890 and 1940. They maintained that "higher education in the United States today [i.e., 1999] has several salient characteristics: the large average size of its institutions; the coexistence of small liberal arts colleges and large research institutions; the substantial share of enrollment in the public sector; a viable and long-lived private sector."[17] In the years after 1890, various substantive trends emerged that helped define and invigorate higher education in the United States. They included the division and subdivision of certain academic disciplines and learned societies into specialized fields; sharp enrollments between 1890 and 1970 (influenced by the growth in the U.S. population); changes in the economics of higher education (especially with state support for state colleges and universities); and "changes in scope," that is an increased emphasis on research and the decline "of independent schools of theology and denominational institutions in general."[18]

THE GROWTH IN HIGHER EDUCATION

Reliable data about higher education enrollments, as of 1870, are available from the U.S. Department of Education (Education), Office of Educational Research and Development (OERD). In 1870, total college enrollments stood at 62,839. In the following years, enrollments grew rather rapidly, reaching 115,850 (+84.36%) in 1880. By 1930, during the Great Depression, enrollments topped the one million mark (1,100,737). The growth rates in the post-war years (1950 to 1970) were astonishing, reaching 8,004,660 in 1970. By 2000, higher education enrollments exceeded the 15 million mark. Overall, higher education in the United States, between 1870 and 2000, posted an impressive growth rate of

Table 1.2   U.S. population 1890–2000 and higher enrollment: 1870–2000

Year	U.S. population	Higher education enrollment
1870	39,818,449	62,839
1880	50,189,209	115,850
1890	62,979,766	158,756
1900	76,212,168	237,592
1910	92,228,531	355,430
1920	106,021,568	597,880
1930	121,202,660	1,100,737
1940	132,165,129	1,494,203
1950	151,325,798	2,444,900
1960	179,323,175	3,639,847
1970	203,211,926	8,004,660
1980	225,545,805	11,569,899
1990	248,799,873	13,819,000
2000	281,421,906	15,312,000
1870–2000 **Percent change**	+606.76%	+24,267.03%

Source: *The Statistical Abstract of the United States 2024*; Table 1; Table 290

N.B. All numbers rounded off. Thomas D. Snyder, editor. *120 Years of American Education: A Statistical Portrait*. Washington, DC: U.S. Department of Education, Office of Educational Research and Improvement, 1990, Table 23. N.B. The higher education data is for the academic year starting in the fall semester 1890, 1900, etc

+24,267.03%. This tally greatly exceeded the total increase in the U.S. population during those same years (+606.76%). Table 1.2 has the data on enrollments and the U.S. population.

Increases in higher education enrollments triggered a growth in the number of courses offered by humanities departments as well as the total number of students majoring in the humanities. In addition, the concept of the importance of the liberal arts, even in the new non-liberal arts colleges, meant that almost every college had distribution requirements for all of their students in the humanities (e.g., requirements to take courses in, for example, English composition, American history, philosophy, etc.).

THE NUMBER OF HUMANITIES MAJORS

Detailed statistical data from the U.S. Department of Education (Education) does not exist for specific college majors in the humanities for the eighteenth century, the nineteenth century, or the early years of the twentieth century. Fortunately, the American Academy of Arts and Sciences (AAAS) has collected data since 1950 about undergraduate and graduate majors in the humanities in six important categories: classical studies, English language and literature, history, linguistics, philosophy, and languages and literature other than in English (i.e. foreign languages, including French, German, etc.). Unfortunately, AAAS did not release data about the other major categories in the humanities (e.g., communications, area studies, etc.).

On the bachelor's degree level, the number of majors in the six humanities areas stood at 38,808 in 1950. The number of majors grew rather slowly by 1960 (43,941, +13.23%). However, the 1960s were a "golden period" for majoring in the humanities, reaching 127,401 by 1970 (+189.94% since 1960). Unfortunately, the total dropped sharply in 1980 to 68,186 (-46.48%; probably because of economic problems in the country), but stronger gains were posted in 1990 (85,760) and 2000, topping 95,756. Overall, the number of bachelor's humanities majors grew an impressive +146.74% between 1950 and 2000.

On the master's level, the number of majors in the humanities grew slowly between 1950 (5389) and 1960 (6242; +15.83%). However, the growth during the 1960s to 1970 (19,483) was exceptionally impressive (+212.13%). Regrettably, declines were posted for 1980 (11,806; -39.40%). Increases were recorded for 1990 (12,259; +3.84%) and 2000 (13,0319; +8.65%). This category's growth rate between 1950 and 2000 (+147.15%) paralleled that of the bachelor's (+146.74%).

The data for doctoral major in the humanities revealed a more steady and impressive increase during 1950 (784), 1960 (1105; +40.94%), and 1970 (3484; +215.29%). This category also sustained a decline in 1980 (3009; -13.63%) and in 1990 (2603; -13.49%). However, 2000 was a better year with a sharp increase (3913; +50.33%). Overall this sector was up +399.11% between 1950 and 2000. Table 1.3 has the data.

In conclusion, the number of majors in the humanities sustained declines after 1970 for the bachelor's and master's and between 1970 and 1980 for doctoral degrees.

Table 1.3 Number of majors in the humanities: 1950–2000

Year	Bachelor	Masters	Doctoral
1950	38,808	5389	784
1960	43,941	6242	1105
1970	127,401	19,483	3484
1980	68,186	11,806	3009
1990	85,760	12,259	2603
2000	95,756	13,319	3913
1950–1970 Percent change	+146.74%	+147.15	+399.11%
1970–2000 Percent change	-24.84%	-31.64%	+12.31%

Source: American Academy of Arts and Sciences. "Bachelor's Degrees in the Humanities"; https://www.amacad.org/humanities-indicators/higher-education/bachelors-degrees-humanities#31600

N.B. The bachelor's, master's, and doctoral degree categories include the following six fields in the humanities: classical studies, English language and literature, history, linguistics, philosophy, and languages and literature other than English. AAAS excluded the other fields in the humanities

THE IMPACT OF SCIENCE AND RECESSIONS ON THE PROMINENCE OF THE HUMANITIES IN HIGHER EDUCATION

Why did the humanities sustain declines in the number of majors after 1970? Clearly, the great scientific research projects that took place during World War II and in the years after 1945 sparked interest among higher education students (as well as academic administrators) in the science, technology, and medical (STM) fields and business administration.[19]

In addition, the dramatic impact of the Russian launch of Sputnik proved to be another reason encouraging students to major in the STM academic field and not in the humanities. The history of the National Science Foundation (NSF) outlined the impact that this Russian satellite had on U.S. society, politics, and science education in the United States. "Sputnik once again elevated the word 'competition' in the language of government officials and the American public. Sputnik threatened the American national interest even more than the Soviet Union's breaking of America's atomic monopoly in 1949; indeed it rocked the very defense of the United States because Russia's ability to place a satellite into orbit meant that it could build rockets powerful enough to propel hydrogen bomb warheads atop intercontinental ballistic missiles. Perhaps more importantly, however, Sputnik forced a national self-appraisal that questioned American education, scientific, technical and industrial strength, and even the moral fiber of the nation. What had gone wrong, questioned the pundits as well as the man in the street. They saw the nation's tradition of being 'Number One' facing its toughest competition, particularly in the areas of science and technology and in science education. With its ties to the nation's research universities, the Foundation of course became a key player in the unfolding events during this trying time. An indication is shown by the large increase in Foundation monies for programs already in place and for new programs. In fiscal year 1958, the year before Sputnik, the Foundation's appropriation had leveled at $40 million. In fiscal 1959, it more than tripled at $134 million, and by 1968 the Foundation budget stood at nearly $500 million. Highlights of this phase of the agency's history cannot be told in a vacuum, however, but must be placed within the broad context of American political happenings. The Congress reacted to Sputnik with important pieces of legislation and an internal reorganization of its own committees. Taken together, the action announced that America would meet the Soviet competition. The National Aeronautics and Space Act, more than any other post-Sputnik law, had great impact on increasing federal funding of scientific research and development. Signed by the president in July 1958, the law created the National Aeronautics and Space Administration (NASA) and gave it responsibility for the technological advancement of the space program. NASA became a major contracting agency and boosted tremendously the extra moral research support of the federal government. NASA not only symbolized America's response to the Soviet challenge, but also dramatized the federal role in support of science and technology."[20]

These developments meant that U.S. higher education institutions had to invest large sums of money into hiring STM faculty members, renovating or building state-of-the-art STM facilities and laboratories, and provide funding for graduate students to conduct research, under the aegis of a faculty member, and/or teach introductory STM courses to students. Many of these STM laboratories and facilities became showcases for visiting parents and potential students (and named facilities for wealthy alumni and donors). Far too many university administrators believed incorrectly that faculty members in history, philosophy, or American literature departments just needed a classroom with a chalk board.

In addition, the passage of the G.I. Bill on June 22, 1944, sparked an increased interest in emphasizing research in the arts and sciences to increase the prestige of a college. This meant that any colleges that wanted to become a major research doctoral university (known as an R1 or an R2) had to comply with the Carnegie Classification of Institutions of Higher Education. "The Basic Classification… includes institutions that awarded at least 20 research/scholarship doctoral degrees during the update year and also institutions with below 20 research/scholarship doctoral degrees that awarded at least 30 professional practice doctoral degrees in at least 2 programs… The first two categories include only institutions that awarded at least 20 research/scholarship doctoral degrees and had at least $5 million in total research expenditures (as reported through the National Science Foundation (NSF) Higher Education Research & Development Survey (HERD)."[21]

As Julius Caesar said when he crossed the Rubicon. *Aleaj jacta est* ("the die is cast; there is no turning back").[22] The quest for funding and prestige meant stressing scientific research; and the historical preeminence of the humanities in U.S. higher education began to change.

Another important trend was the impact of recessions. While there were 13 U.S. recessions since February 1945, many undergraduate and graduate students began to consider majors that were useful in getting a job. This explains why certain academic fields, for example business administration (especially finance and marketing), economics, and information science, experienced a growth in undergraduate and graduate school enrollments in the years after 1970. Table 1.4 has a list of the recessions, the start and stop date for the recessions, and the high point in the unemployment rates during these recessions.

Table 1.4 Economic recessions in the United States since 1945

Start	End	Duration	Peak unemployment rate
February 1945	October 1945	8 months	5.2%
November 1948	October 1949	11 months	7.9%
July 1953	May 1954	10 months	6.1%
August 1957	April 1958	8 months	7.5%
April 1960	February 1961	10 months	7.1%
December 1969	November 1970	11 months	6.1%
November 1973	March 1975	16 months	9.0%
January 1980	July 1980	6 months	7.8%
July 1981	November 1982	16 months	10.8%
July 1990	March 1991	8 months	7.8%
March 2001	November 2001	8 months	6.3%
December 2007	June 2009	18 months	10.0%
February 2020	April 2020	2 months	14.7%

Source: National Bureau of Economic Research (NBER). "U.S. Business Cycle Expansions and Contractions"; https://www.nber.org/research/data/us-business-cycle-expansions-and-contractions

CONCLUSION

In spite of the growth in interest and prestige of the STM and business academic fields, the humanities remained important because they provided an intellectual framework that was of pivotal importance to every undergraduate regardless of major. This is why many colleges had distribution (i.e., mandatory) requirements in the humanities.

Clearly, the humanities will never disappear from junior or community colleges or four-year institutions. But the preeminence of the humanities by 2000 had receded from where it had been just a few decades before 2000.

NOTES

1. Merriam-Webster Dictionary. "Humanities;" https://www.merriam-webster.com/dictionary/humanity#:~:text=y%C3%BC%2D-,plural%20 humanities,concerned%20primarily%20with%20human%20culture.
2. Merriam-Webster Dictionary. "Philosophy;" https://www.merrianwebster.com/dictionary/philosophy.
3. Ted Levitt's "Marketing Myopia;" https://hbr.org/2004/07/marketing-myopia.
4. The British Library. "William Caxton;" https://www.bl.uk/people/william-caxton. Also see The Library of Congress. "The Gutenberg Bible;" https://www.loc.gov/exhibits/bibles/the-gutenberg-bible.html; Museum of Printing. "Gutenberg and the History of the Printing of the Printed Bible:" https://museumofprinting.org/news-and-events/guten berg-and-the-history-of-the-printed-bible.
5. Oxford University Press. "About Oxford University Press' History;" https://global.oup.com/about/oup_history/?cc=us.
6. Ernesto Spinak and Abel L. Parker, "350 Years of Scientific Publications from the *Journal des Scavans* and *Philosophical Transactions* to SciELO;" https://blog.scielo.org/en/2015/03/05/350-years-of-scientific-publication-from-the-journal-des-scavans-and-philosophical-transactions-to-scielo. Also see Albert N. Greco. *The Strategic Marketing of Science, Technology, and Medical Journals: A Business History of a Dynamic Marketplace, 2000–2020* (Cham, Switzerland: Palgrave Macmillan, 2023, pp. 1–24.
7. Aileen Fyfe, Julie McDougall-Waters, and Noah Moxham, "350 Years of Scientific Periodicals;" https://royalsociwetypublishing.org/doi/10. 1098/rsnr.2015.
8. American Philosophical Society (APS). "About the APS;" https://www.amphilsoc.org/about.

9. Charles Homer Haskins. The Rise of *Universities* (Ithaca, NY: Cornnell University Press, 1972); pp. 17–129.
10. Susquehanna University. "A Brief History of American Higher Education: Part One Colonial Colleges;" http://www.susquehannapresidentsblog. com/2021/07/a-brief-history-of-american-higher-education. Also see John R. Thelin. *A History of American Higher Education* (Baltimore, MD: Johns Hopkins University Press, 2019); pp. 21–83. Lawrence Cremin. *American Education: The Colonial Experience, 1607–1783* (New York: Harper & Row, 1970), pp. 36–179. Bernard Bailyn. *Education in the Forming of American Society* (Chapel Hill, NC University of North Education Carolina Press, 1960), 15–71.
11. Roger L. Geiger. *The History of American Higher Education: Learning and Culture from the Founding to World War II* (Princeton: Princeton University Press, 2015), pp. 33–122, 173–268.
12. The National Archives. "Morrill Act (1862);" https://www.senate.gov/ artandhistory/history/common/civil_war/MorrillLandGrant CollegeAct_FeaturedDoc.htm#:~:text=First%20proposed%20when%20 Morrill%20was,law%20on%20July%202%2C%201862.
13. Geiger. *The History of American Higher Education: Learning and Culture from the Founding to World War II*, pp. 269–314.
14. Emily A. Langdon. "Women's Colleges Then and Now: Access Then, Equity Now," *Peabody Journal of Education 76*, 1(2001): 5–30.
15. Marybeth Gasman. *Envisioning Black Colleges: A History of the United Negro College Fund* (Baltimore, MD: Johns Hopkins University Press, 2007), pp. 46–177.
16. Robert Bruce Slater. "The Blacks Who First Entered the World of White Higher Education," *The Journal of Blacks in Higher Education*, 4(Summer 1994): 47–56.
17. Claudia Goldin and Lawrence F. Katz. "The Shaping of Higher Education: The Formative Years in the United States, 1890–1940," *Journal of Economic Perspective 13*, 1(Winter 1999): 37.
18. Ibid., pages 38, 44–45.
19. Albert N. Greco. *The Growth of the Scholarly Publishing Industry in the U.S.: A Business History of a Changing Marketplace* (Cham, Switzerland: Palgrave Macmillan, 2019), pp. 11–84. Also see Greco. *The Marketing of World War II in the U.S., 1949–1946: A Business History of the U.S. Government and the Media and Entertainment Industries* (Cham, Switzerland: Palgrave Macmillan, 2020), pp.13–30. Greco. *The Strategic Marketing of Science, Technology, and Medical Journals: A Business History of a Dynamic Marketplace, 2000–2020* (Cham, Switzerland: Palgrave Macmillan, 2020), pp. 1–24, 47–68.

20. The National Science Foundation. "The National Science Foundation: A Brief History;" https://www.nsf.gov/about/history/nsf50/nsf8816.jsp.
21. The Carnegie Commission on Higher Education. "The Carnegie Classification of Institutions of Higher Education;" https://carnegieclassifications.acenet.edu/carnegie-classification/classification-methodology/basic-classification.
22. Merriam-Webster Dictionary. "*Alea jacta est*, Latin quotation from Julius Caesar:" https://www.merriam-webster.com/dictionary/alea%20jacta%20est.

CHAPTER 2

The State of the Humanities and Scholarly Publishing to 2000

Abstract The first book printed in the United States was *The Bay Psalm Book* in 1640. The first scholarly journal was published in Europe in 1665. In England, there were university presses at Oxford (1478) and Cambridge (1534) before there were learned societies. The opposite was the case in the United States. The first university press was created only in 1869 at Cornell University, and this press closed operations after a few years. The next university press was at Johns Hopkins University. Eventually, other university presses were launched publishing humanities books. By the mid-twentieth century, commercial scholarly presses challenged the preeminent position of university presses in humanities publishing. This chapter analyzed the creation of societies, and the growth and perils university presses confronted.

Keywords *The Bay Psalm Book* • Early publishing in the U.S. Societies • Scholarly journals • Scholarly books • Scholarly book profit and loss statement • University presses • Commercial scholarly publishers • Trade books • American Library Association • Serials crisis

A. N. Greco, *Scholarly Publishing in the Humanities, 2000–2024*, Marketing and Communication in Higher Education, https://doi.org/10.1007/978-3-031-66170-9_2

THE EARLY YEARS OF THE U.S. BOOK PUBLISHING INDUSTRY

In 1640 a printing press was imported from England to Cambridge, MA, the type invented by Gutenberg in Germany. The press was operated manually, and the lead type was set by hand. A piece of paper was printed one sheet at a time, and the inked paper had to dry before a collection of printed pages could be pieced together (called a "signature") and bound into a book.[1] This small press printed the first book that is now in the United States; it was *The Bay Psalm Book.*[2]

By 1685, Philadelphia was publishing all types of reading materials, and Benjamin Franklin operated a printing and publishing operation in that city.[3] By 1693, New York City witnessed the start of its publishing history.[4] However, New York City emerged eventually as the center of book publishing in the United States. In essence, book publishing in New York became what economists and marketers called an "industry cluster" (sometimes called a "competitive cluster" or a "Porterian cluster," named after Michael E. Porter, the Harvard business scholar). Porter maintained that an "industry cluster" allows companies to increase productivity because of the availability of what economists call "agglomeration," that is a geographical "cluster" that effectively attracted enough key personnel to New York. A "book cluster" enabled a publishing firm to create and launch new operations (perhaps an imprint centered on publishing serious literary fiction) because of relatively low or at least reasonable costs.[5]

THE DEVELOPMENT AND IMPACT OF SCHOLARLY SOCIETIES AND SCHOLARLY JOURNALS ON PUBLISHING IN THE HUMANITIES

Aside from the first journal published in France in January 1665, the majority of scholarly journals published in England and in Europe were by learned and professional societies. Some of the important English society journals include *A Literary Journal* (1746), the *Monthly Review* (1774), the *London Medical Journal* (1781), the *Journal of Natural Philosophy* and *Chemistry, and the Arts* (In 1791), *A Christian Journal* (1792), the *Mining Journal* (1840), the *British Medical Journal* (1840), the *Journal of Ecology* (1913).[6]

This pattern was replicated, for the most part in the American colonies and especially after the creation of the United States. Benjamin Franklin founded the American Philosophical Society (APS) in colonial Philadelphia in 1743. APS is "the oldest learned society in the United States... [created]

for the purpose of 'promoting useful knowledge'." The APS has published the "Transactions of the American the Philosophical Society" since 1771.[7] In 1780, the American Academy of Arts and Sciences (AAAS) was created in Cambridge Massachusetts by a group of the Founding Fathers of the United States, including John Adams and John Hancock. The AAAS *"honors excellence and convenes leaders from every field of human endeavor to examine new ideas, address issues of importance to the nation and the world, and work together 'to cultivate every art and science which may tend to advance the interest, honor, dignity, and happiness of a free, independent, and virtuous people.'"* AAAS has published the scholarly journal *Daedalus* since 1846.[8]

Over the years, a number of other learned and professional societies were launched in the United States. Some of the interesting ones created in the nineteenth century include the American Antiquarian Society (created in 1812), the Society for Classical Studies (1869), the Society for Biblical Studies (1880), the Modern Language Association (1883), the American Historical Association (1884), and the American Society of Church History (1881). As could be expected, there was a plethora of societies created in the early years of the twentieth century, including the American Philosophical Association (1900), the Classical Association of the Middle West and South (1905), and the American Academy of Religion (1909).

In the years after the end of World War I, there was an impressive burst of energy to create new societies. Some of the important ones include the American Catholic Historical Association, the American Classical League, and the American Council of Learned Societies (all created in 1919). The war and post-war years also witnessed a number of important societies, including the Association for Asian Studies (1941), the American Musicological Society (1942), the Renaissance Society of America (1954), and the Society for Medieval and Renaissance Philosophy (1978). Table 2.1 has a selective list of these societies back in 1743.

Some of the important scholarly journals released by societies included *Science* (1848), the *Journal of the American Medical Association* (in 1883), the *American Journal of Philology* (1885), *Physical Review* (1893), the *Journal of Economic Literature*, the *American Journal of Botany* (1914), the *American Archivist* (1938), *CA: A Cancer Journal for Clinicians* (1950; the highest ranked journal in the world in 2024), and the *Journal of Cognitive Research* and *Cell* (both in 1974). Some journals were published by individuals including the highly ranked *New England Journal of Medicine* (1812).

Table 2.1 The development of societies in the United States since 1743

Year created	The name of the society
1743	American Philosophical Society
1780	American Academy of Arts and Sciences
1812	American Antiquarian Society
1817	New York Academy of Sciences
1839	American Statistical Association
1848	American Association for the Advancement of Science
1863	National Academy of Sciences
1869	Society for Classical Studies
1879	Archaeological Institute of America
1880	Society of Biblical Literature
1883	Modern Language Association
1884	American Historical Association
1885	American Economic Association
1888	American Mathematical Society
1888	American Society of Church History
1888	Geological Society of America
1888	National Geographic Society
1897	American Medical Association
1899	American Academy of Arts and Letters
1899	American Astronomical Society
1899	American Physical Society
1900	American Philosophical Association
1904	American Association of Geographers
1905	Classical Association of the Middle West and South
1906	Classical Association of New England
1909	American Academy of Religion
1911	College Art Association
1919	American Catholic Historical Association
1919	American Classical League
1919	American Council of learned Societies
1919	American Geophysical Union
1919	American Meteorological Society
1940	Society of Architectural Historians
1941	Association for Asian Studies
1942	American Musicological Society
1942	American Society for Aesthetics
1947	Bibliographical Society of the University of Virginia
1954	The Renaissance Society of America
1966	Middle East Studies Association of North America
1967	Society for Historians of American Foreign Relations
1977	Society for Music Theory
1978	Society for Medieval and Renaissance Philosophy

Source: The American Council of Learned Societies. "Member Societies;" https://www.acls.org/acls-members-societies; and society websites

N.B. This is a selective list of societies

SCHOLARLY JOURNALS IN THE HUMANITIES

While reliable statistical data is available for books, there is a major issue regarding obtaining detailed information about scholarly journals in the humanities. The *Bowker Annual* and the *Library and Book Trade Almanac* (the name of the *Bowker Annual* was changed to the *Library and Book Trade Almanac* in 2008) have statistical data about all types of books; however, these generally reliable reference works have incomplete journal data for the years before 1980 and through the 1990s.

The American Library Association (ALA) only started to list some journal stats in the 1980s. The first year of ALA scholarly journal information is for 1984. For example, the ALA's journal category "general and humanities" (the term they employed for humanities journals) lists important data for 1984, but there is no data listed for 1985, 1986, or 1987.

In 1984, there were 1537 scholarly journals listed on the ALA website. Of that number, there were 122 in the "humanities and general" journal category (7.94% of the total). The other major categories were larger than the "humanities and general" journals: science and technology had 284 journals (18.28%); the social sciences, 159 (10.24%); and business, 289 (18.80%). Detailed information about specific journal categories in the humanities (e.g., philosophy, religion, American literature, etc.) was not available from the ALA. However, data is available in Table 2.2 for the years 1984 to 2000 for the "general and humanities" sector.

However, there is an abundance of scholarly journals in the humanities. Some of the important ones include the *American Journal of Archeology* (launched in 1897), the *Papers of the Bibliographical Society of America* (1913), the *Journal of American History* (1913), the *American Archivist* (1938), the *Studies in Bibliography* (1949), *New Media and Society* (1949), *Modern Fiction Studies* (1955), *Journal of the History of Philosophy* (1963), and *American Literary History* (1989).

Reliable data was available for only a selected number of years. However, looking at the years after 1984 in Table 2.3, the total number of titles in the humanities listed in the ALA dataset declined by five titles (-4.10%) between 1984 and 2000. However, the average prices for the "general and humanities" journal sector posted exceptionally large annual increases, +155.35% between 1984 (when it was $196.60) and 2000 (in that year the average price skyrocketed to $503.98).

According to the U.S. Department of Labor (Labor), Bureau of Labor Statistics (BLS), the U.S. Consumer Price Index (CPI) for all urban

Table 2.2 Number of scholarly journals: 1984–2000

Year	Number of titles				
	All serials	General and humanities	Science and technology	Social sciences	Business
1984	1537	122	281	159	289
1985–1987	N/A	N/A	N/A	N/A	N/A
1988	1310	116	302	154	281
1989	1308	116	302	154	281
1990	1308	116	303	156	281
1991	1307	116	302	156	281
1992	1294	116	301	154	278
1993	1294	116	301	154	278
1994	1294	116	301	154	275
1995	1280	116	301	154	281
1996	1280	116	301	154	281
1997	1281	115	302	151	287
1998	1282	115	307	152	287
1999	1286	115	301	152	294
2000	1294	117	299	152	297
1984–2000 Percent change	-15.81%	-4.10%	+6.41%	-4.40%	+2.77%

Source: Nancy J. Chaffin. The American Library Association (ALA). "U.S. Serial Services Price Index for 2000"; https://alair.ala.org/bitstream/handle/11213/460/serials00.pdf?sequence=1&isAllowed=y
N.B.: ALA tracks annually a selective list of scholarly journals. Not every journal category is listed in this table

consumers increased by +38.9% between 1989 and 2000.[9] Clearly, journal price increases of this magnitude triggered concern in the academic community, and this situation became known as the "serials crisis" since the journal budgets at many academic and research libraries failed to keep pace with these sharp increases. For example, the price increase for many of the other categories grew at what some journal observers viewed as "alarming rates," including science and technology, +193.44%; business administration, +87.78%; the eclectic social sciences, +111.42%; and legal journals, +155.63%. All of the data can be found in Table 2.4.

Table 2.3 The price of scholarly journals in the "General and Humanities" category: 1984–2000

Year	Number of titles	Average price	Annual percent price change
1984	122	$196.60	N/A
1985–1987	N/A	N/A	N/A
1988	116	$225.95	N/A
1989	116	$255.27	+13.00%
1990	116	$274.39	+7.50%
1991	116	$292.23	+6.50%
1992	116	$317.15	+8.50%
1993	116	$336.71	+6.20%
1994	116	$362.25	+7.60%
1995	116	$381.80	+5.40%
1996	116	$410.75	+7.60%
1997	115	$429.12	+4.50%
1998	115	$455.78	+6.20%
1999	115	$492.59	+8.10%
2000	117	$503.98	+2.30%
1984–2000 Percent change	-4.10%	+155.35%	–

Source: Nancy J. Chaffin. The American Library Association (ALA). "U.S. Serial Services Price Index for 2000." https://alair.ala.org/bitstream/handle/11213/460/serials00.pdf?sequence=1&isAllowed=y
N.B. The prices are the suggested prices; discounts were not available

THE PRICE OF SCHOLARLY JOURNALS AND BOOKS IN THE HUMANITIES

The price of six major categories of scholarly journals and books in the humanities was available for the years 1989–2000, including philosophy, religion, history of North America, philology and linguistics, classical languages and literature, and American literature.

As for journals, the average price of five scholarly journals increased at rather modest rates during those years, versus the +38.9% increase in the CPI, including philosophy (+13.76%), history of North America (+20.94%), philology and linguistics (+14.78%), classical languages and literature (+23.56%), and American literature (+19.34). The increase in religion (+66.92%) was quite large, with its average annual cost exceeding $51.93 in 2000, the highest among the six categories. Table 2.5 has the details.

Table 2.4 The price of scholarly journals in the business, science and technology, social sciences, and law: 1984–2000

Year	Business	Science and technology	Social sciences	Law
1984	$437.07	$295.36	$283.82	$275.23
1985–1987	N/A	N/A	N/A	N/A
1988	$458.33	$378.37	$343.18	$338.13
1989	$493.23	$420.15	$345.10	$354.32
1990	$523.79	$443.36	$370.40	$390.98
1991	$584.93	$483.90	$398.76	$424.68
1992	$625.67	$529.35	$420.24	$467.27
1993	$641.28	$560.45	$448.88	$490.44
1994	$676.44	$593.73	$466.86	$504.86
1995	$695.88	$640.14	$487.16	$542.73
1996	$737.14	$675.82	$513.08	$593.81
1997	$751.99	$716.95	$536.85	$592.84
1998	$781.33	$757.33	$557.34	$611.71
1999	$798.73	$804.40	$577.89	$668.61
2000	$820.73	$866.69	$600.06	$703.56
1984–2000 Percent change	+87.78%	+193.44%	+111.42%	+155.63

Source: Nancy J. Chaffin. The American Library Association (ALA). "U.S. Serial Services Price Index for 2000." https://alair.ala.org/bitstream/handle/11213/460/serials00.pdf?sequence=1&isAllowed=y
N.B. The prices are the suggested prices; discounts were not available

In the six book categories, a different pattern was evident. Philology and linguistics (+18.63%), classical languages and literature (+17.74%), and American literature (+30.27%), all posted increases below the increase in the CPI. Religion (+36.6%) and history of North America (+39.57%) all hovered near the CPI's increase. Philosophy (+120.07%) outpaced all of the other book categories especially with rather high average annual suggested prices between 1995 ($73.48) and 2000 ($97.03). Table 2.6 has the details.

COMPETITION IN THE SCHOLARLY PUBLISHING SECTOR: AMERICAN UNIVERSITY PRESSES

In England, there were university presses at Oxford (1478) and Cambridge (1534) before there were learned societies. The opposite was the case in the United States. Almost 400 years after the creation of the university press at Oxford, a small press was created in 1869 at Cornell University.[10] Cornell's

Table 2.5   The price of university press books in the humanities: 1989–2000 (U.S. dollars)

Year	Philosophy	Religion	History of North America	Philology & linguistics	Classical languages & literature	American literature
1989	$35.17	$31.11	$30.75	$35.85	$36.08	$22.85
1990	$38.33	$36.72	$27.56	$34.87	$38.22	$25.37
1991	$42.88	$38.38	$30.41	$44.69	$44.64	$27.07
1992	$40.92	$36.64	$30.04	$41.50	$58.10	$26.82
1993	$36.27	$33.80	$29.88	$38.39	$41.53	$26.04
1994	$35.04	$33.97	$28.72	$37.00	$40.38	$24.12
1995	$36.06	$35.16	$28.84	$40.45	$38.43	$24.90
1996	$36.93	$34.58	$30.77	$39.64	$41.96	$25.48
1997	$37.63	$33.95	$32.68	$41.99	$45.74	$26.72
1998	$40.45	$41.72	$32.12	$43.21	$46.80	$25.85
1999	$40.06	$36.63	$32.62	$42.07	$43.37	$25.87
2000	$40.01	$51.93	$37.19	$41.15	$44.58	$27.04
1989–2000 Percent change	+13.76%	+66.92%	+20.94%	+14.78%	+23.56%	+18.34%

Source: Albert N. Greco, Walter F. O'Connor, Sharon P. Smith, and Robert M. Wharton. "The Price of University Press Books: 1989–2000," *Journal of Scholarly Publishing 35,* 1(October 2003): 4–39
N.B. These are average prices; discounts were not available. This is a selective list
Other averages for the humanities were available in the article

experiment in scholarly publishing sustained a series of setbacks, and it closed operation. The next university press was launched eight years later at Johns Hopkins University, and this press was able to survive in what was a difficult economic environment.[11]

Hopkins' success sparked the interest at other universities, and a number of new presses emerged by the end of the nineteenth century, including Pennsylvania (in 1890), Chicago (1891), Columbia (1893), and California and Northwestern (both in 1893). Eventually in the twentieth century, presses were created at a number of universities, including Catholic University, Duke, Fordham, Harvard, Indiana, Iowa, MIT, Temple, Princeton, Yale, etc.[12] The initial emphasis at many of these presses was on scholarly books, monographs that appealed to faculty members and students. Eventually, a number of presses ventured into scholarly journal publishing since they could predict journal subscriptions, primarily at academic and large research

Table 2.6 The price of professional scholarly publisher books in the humanities: 1989–2000 (U.S. dollars)

Year	Philosophy	Religion	History of North America	Philology & linguistics	Classical languages & literature	American literature
1989	$44.09	$28.74	$29.01	$54.96	$41.65	$17.87
1990	$45.78	$31.85	$33.95	$54.00	$41.22	$19.75
1991	$51.13	$30.53	$36.24	$63.14	$46.89	$19.40
1992	$58.90	$33.19	$29.93	$66.23	$60.20	$20.03
1993	$66.53	$33.56	$33.33	$76.48	$41.80	$19.19
1994	$62.06	$32.01	$32.57	$63.75	$43.66	$19.84
1995	$73.48	$36.49	$32.45	$62.49	$69.27	$19.99
1996	$105.38	$39.27	$32.02	$71.90	$44.71	$21.06
1997	$75.74	$35.90	$35.36	$66.14	$59.56	$21.39
1998	$84.76	$40.54	$39.44	$67.95	$59.46	$22.46
1999	$66.30	$37.90	$39.51	$74.71	$69.21	$22.24
2000	$97.03	$40.12	$40.49	$65.20	$49.04	$23.28
1989–2000 Percent change	+120.07%	+39.60%	+39.57%	+18.63%	+17.74%	+30.27%

Source: Albert N. Greco, Walter F. O'Connor, Sharon P. Smith, and Robert M. Wharton. "The Price of University Press Books: 1989–2000," *Journal of Scholarly Publishing 35*, 1(October 2003): 4–39
N.B. These are average prices; discounts were not available. This is a selective list
Other averages for the humanities were available in the article

libraries, more effectively than the prediction of the sale of a monograph. Some of the important journal publishers include Chicago, Hopkins, and California.

COMPETITION FROM TRADE AND COMMERCIAL SCHOLARLY PUBLISHERS

Trade houses had been active publishers of books in the humanities since the eighteenth century. As they grew in size and importance, in the years after 1980 the major trade operations (specifically, Penguin Random House Simon & Schuster, HarperCollins, Hachette, and Macmillan) expanded into the humanities sectors by creating or increasing their lists in the humanities. Dan Sinykin wrote about the financial troubles at Simon & Schuster (S & S). Richard Snyder, S & S's CEO "perceived trade publishing alone was too volatile for a public company... You cannot get the growth necessary to meet the [financial] standards of a parent like Paramount... [S & S] was grinding out anything [i.e., different types of books] that will improve the bottom line."[13] S & S was not alone at evaluating the prospects of adding or increasing a humanities list.

Commercial scholarly publishers had existed for years. However, in the years after 1970, and especially in the 1980s and 1990s, they became far more active in the scholarly book publishing sector in the United States and abroad. Some of the important publishers included Elsevier (also known as RELX), Wolters Kluwer, Sage, John Wiley, Informa, Springer Nature, and Brill.

Major Developments and Theories That Impacted Scholarly Publishing in the Humanities

Al Silverman in his remarkable book *The Time of Their Lives: The Golden Age of Great American Publishers, Their Editors, and Authors* remarked that "I determined that the golden age [of book publishing] had to be the years from 1946, as the harrowing savagery of World War II was washing away, to the late 1970s and early 1980s, before the era of publishing ossification had fully set in. Ossification had begun in the 1960s when the great old-line book people began to be replaced by bottom-line businessmen."[14]

Silverman was correct. In the years mainly after 1980, a series of events and business developments emerged that transformed the humanities and the publication and availability of books and journal articles in the humanities. Some of these developments include the following.

First, scholarly book publishing and especially in the journal area grew in size and importance with the adoption of basic business theories and strategies, and the development and emergence of significant global markets, especially in Eastern Europe, Asia, Central and South America, and Africa.[15] Scholars in those regions wanted access to the latest theories and research findings published in scholarly books and journal articles in the humanities. Many of these publishing operations opened offices in these regions (e.g., Oxford University Press).[16]

In essence, the large book and journal publishers realized that Ted Levitt was correct. In order to grow and survive in a rather demanding scholarly publishing environment, they had to become market oriented and not product oriented. Levitt, writing in the *Harvard Business Review*

(*HBR*), maintained in his exceptionally important article "Marketing Myopia" that "there is no such thing as a growth industry. I believe there are only companies organized and operated to create and capitalize on growth opportunities."[17] This meant that a company had to understand that the purpose of a business was to recognize, understand, and satisfy the needs of a customer. So, a publisher of scholarly books or journals in the humanities had to create and maintain an effective marketing environment; in essence, to make sure that every employee was market, and not product, oriented; and that marketing was the job of every employee.[18]

Augmenting the theories of Ted Levitt was the innovative research of Michael E. Porter. Porter, also writing in the HBR, developed a marketing methodology in his key article "The Five Forces That Shape Strategy." To Porter, an effective executive seeks to develop a competitive edge, in essence a unique value advantage, over rival firms through the adoption and utilization of the "five forces," which include understanding: (1) competitive rivalry; (2) supplier power, (3) buyer power, (4) the threat of substation, and (5) the threat of new entry into the market.[19]

This meant that publishers came to grips with the reality that their information content in the humanities had value in the marketplace of academics, general readers, and libraries. After all, in almost every instance, they owned the copyright for the material they published. However, publishers incurred costs, and, in many instances substantial costs, related to their expenditures for plant (i.e., editorial, art, design, layout; and page make-up); printing, paper, and binding (PPB); warehousing, sales, marketing, internet archiving of content, and the distribution of printed and digital content); and, in the case of books, returns for full credit. So, these publishing operations became more efficient, and they initiated procedures to capitalize on extracting a return on their investments.

Second, academic, public, government, and special libraries have always been a major purchaser of scholarly books and journals in the humanities. What occurred during the years after 1990 has been called the "serials crisis," that is sharp increases in the annual subscription costs for serials. However, the largest increases were clearly in the scientific, technical, and medicine (STM) category of journals. For example, the average cost of a chemistry journal in 1998 was $1218.00, $1306.00 in 1999, and $1442.00 in 2000. Physics journals during those same years were also high (1998: $1263.00; 1999: $1389.00; 2000: $1508.00).[20]

Unfortunately, many libraries' budgets could not keep pace with the increase in STM journals, triggering the creation of the "serials crisis."

Many libraries began to cancel journal subscriptions. "Academic libraries were cancelling journals unique to their collections and other collections."[21] Canceling journals was a last resort since it impacted negatively academics and students who needed access to certain journals. Emily R. Mobley, the university librarian at Purdue University, remarked that "'the sins of the past' coupled with the myopia of not looking outside the ivied walls of academe provided the foundation of the current crisis... Often I've heard the comment from university administrators that the serials crisis is a library problem... I take great delight in telling them 'Au contraire,' it's your problem...The faculty have a unique role in that they are both creators and consumers of the [scholarly journal] products."[22] Very preliminary discussions took place in Europe about the need to have free (i.e., "open access" (OA)) journals; academics in the United States began to pay attention to these European discussions.

Third, regardless of whether the well-entrenched, widespread publish or perish policies at most universities or the fact that commercial publishers had stockholders who expected a return on their investment, a growing number of academics blamed publishers, and they responded by supporting the launch of digital operations. The rapid, innovative developments in technology allowed academics the opportunity to utilize large computers, and later portable laptops and tablets, to save research work originally on disks and later on the computer. The emergence of and expansion of the internet enabled academics to share content with researchers in other regions and countries, effectively opening the door for online only publications (e.g., in 1990 *Postmodern Culture* was created as an online only publication) or on pre-print servers (e.g., in 1991 arXiv became a significant site for scientists and mathematicians). These successes triggered the creation of the Public Library of Science (PLOS) in 2003.

Fourth, hope springs eternal, and the critics of the publishers rarely, if ever, addressed the costs to publish and disseminate scholarly books or journals in the humanities (much less scholarly output in STM or the social sciences). Table 2.7 has a sample (i.e., a representative) profit and loss (P & L) statement for a paperback history book (about the New Deal 1933–1941) published by a university press. The publisher had high hopes for this book, and 2000 copies were printed. However, it is important to understand the economics of scholarly book publishing, which can be daunting at times.

The key economic issues in this P & L are as follows. The 2000 print run was reduced by the 100 free copies (given to the authors, sales reps, the editorial team, etc.), 266 copies never shipped, and 359 copies shipped and were returned. So, this title had net sales of 1275 copies. This book had a suggested retail price (SRP) of $40.00, and the book was sold to various retailers (bookstores and online sites) at a 48% discount, netting the publisher $20.80 for each sold copy.

The costs to produce the books were as follows. Printing, paper, and binding (PPB): $7000 ($3.50 for each book's PPB for 2000 copies); plant (editorial, art, design, layout, and page makeup): $1000; marketing: $1000; author's advance $0 (the author was paid a 10% royalty on net sales; i.e., $2.80 per copy). The book did not have any reprint or subsidiary income. The book's income was $26,520 (i.e., 1275 copies at $20.80 each).

The total cost of goods sold (COGS): $10,652. The initial gross margin was $15,868; the inventory write-off of $2500 reduced the initial gross margin to $13,368 (the final gross margin). Corporate charges (marketing: $1000; and corporate overhead $5304 (20% of net sales)) reduced the book's net profit to $7064.

This was a successful book with very good reviews in various scholarly journals, and it generated a small profit for this university press which allocated a substantial amount of time and expense. However, far too many books in the humanities fail to sell these many copies and generate a +26.64% net profit as a percentage of net sales. Table 2.7 has the details.

CONCLUSION

In spite of certain disconcerting developments, the humanities scholarly journal and scholarly book publishing industry was poised in 2000 for what many publishing executives believed were years of impressive substantial growth in this eclectic, often unpredictable, business that started when Matthew Day (sometimes written as Daye) printed and sold all 1700 copies of America's first "bestseller," *The Bay Psalm Book*.

Table 2.7   Sample profit and loss (P & L) University Press printed paper-back book

Assumptions

256-page black and white printed paperback book; no photographs, no illustrations, and 51 statistical tables

Print run	2000 copies	[256-page book, no photos]
Free copies	100 copies	[author, editor, publishing house]
Gross sales	1900 copies	
Never shipped	266 copies	[14%]
Returns	359 copies	[21.97% return rate; 22% is the average return rate for this type of university press paperback books]
Net sales	1275 copies	[67.11% sell through rate]
Suggested retail price	$40.00	
Average discount	48%	[$20.80 net to publisher]
Unit PPB	$7000.00	[@$3.50 × 2000 copies; PPB done in Asia]
Plant	$1000.00	[some work done in Asia]
Marketing	$1000.00	
Author's advance	$0	[Royalty rate: 10% of net to publisher; @$2.08 per copy]
Other publishing income		
Sub. Rights		

	Gross	Author's percent	Publishers' percent
Reprints	0	0	0
Book club	$0	50% [$0]	50% [$0]
1st serial	$0	90% [$0]	10% [$0]
2nd serial	$0	30% [$0]	70% [$0]
Total	$0	50% [$0]	50% [$0]
Revenues			
1.	Print run:	2000	
1a.	House-author copies:	100	
1b.	Print run minus house-author:	1900	
2a.	Copies returned:	359	

(*continued*)

Table 2.7 (continued)

Assumptions			
256-page black and white printed paperback book; no photographs, no illustrations, and 51 statistical tables			
2b.	Total copies never shipped:	266	
2c.	Total copies sold:	1275	
3.	Net sales:	$26,520	[#1b – #2a – #2b = #2c] [@$20.80 × 1275 copies = $26,520]
Cost of goods sold (COGS)			
4.	Plant	$1000.00	
5.	PPB	$7000.00	[2000 × $3.50]
6.	Royalty	$2652.00	[10% net to publisher; $2.08; 1275 units × $2.08 = $2652.00]
7.	Royalty write-off:	$0	
8.	Total COGS	$10,652.00	[#4 + #5 + #6 + #7 = #8]
	Initial gross margin	$15,868.00	[#3 – #8 = #9]
9.	Other publishing income:	$0	
10.	Final gross margin:	$15,868.00	[#9 – #10 = #11]
	Inventory w/o	$2500.00	[@$4.00 × 625 copies] PPB $7000.00 + Plant $1000.00 = $8000.00 divided by 2000 copies = $4.00 per copy; 359 returns + 266 never shipped = 625 copies

(*continued*)

Table 2.7 (continued)

Assumptions			
256-page black and white printed paperback book; no photographs, no illustrations, and 51 statistical tables			
11.	Final groass margin - inventor w/o	$13,368.00	
Corporate Charges			
12.	Marketing:	$1000.00	
13.	Overhead 20%	$5304.00	[20% of net sales]
14.	Net profit	$7064.00	[#11 - #12 - #13 = #14.] [Net profit as a % of net sales = 26.64%]

NOTES

1. Elizabeth Eisenstein. *The Printing Revolution in Early Modern Europe* (Cambridge: Cambridge University Press, 2012), pages 20–115. Also see Elizabeth L. Eisenstein, *The Printing Press as an Agent of Change (Volumes 1 and 2 in One)* (Cambridge: Cambridge University Press, 1980), 22–182; Elizabeth L. Eisenstein, *The Printing Revolution in Early Modern Europe* (Cambridge: Cambridge University Press, 2012), 78–115; Jeremiah E. Dittmar, "Information Technology and Economic Change: The Impact of the Printing Press," *Quarterly Journal of Economics* 126 (2011): 1133–1172. Christopher de Hamel. *The Manuscript Club* (New York: Penguin Press, 2023), 13–86.

2. Amy M.E. Morris. "The Art of Purifying: The Bay Psalm Book and Colonial Puritanism," *Early American Literature* 42, 1(2007): 107–130. Also see Hugh Amory, "Printing and Bookselling in New England, 1638–1713," in Hugh Amory and David D. Hall, eds. *A History of the Book in America, Vol. 1 The Colonial Book in the Atlantic World* (Cambridge, U.K.: Cambridge University Press, 2000), pages 83–116; Perry Miller. *The New England Mind: The Seventeenth Century* (Cambridge: Harvard University Press, 1954), pages 73–90; Hugh Amory. " 'Gods Altar Needs Not Our Pollishings:' Revisiting the *Bay Psalm Book*." *Printing History* 12 (1990): 2–14. Hugh Amory, "Printing and Bookselling in New England, 1638–1713," in Hugh Amory and David D. Hall, eds. *A History of the*

Book in America, Vol. 1 The Colonial Book in the Atlantic World, page 106. Of The Bay Psalm Book's original print run of 1700 copies, printed in quarto on a letterpress press, only 11 copies are known still to exist, and only 5 are complete copies of the book. On November 26, 2013, "at Sotheby's New York, one of only 11 surviving copies of The Bay Psalm Book set a then new world auction record for any printed book when it sold for $14,165,000. The book was purchased by American businessman and philanthropist David Rubenstein, who plans to share it with the American public by loaning it to libraries across the country, before putting it on long-term loan at one of them," http://www.sothebys.com/en/auctions/2013/the-bay-psalm-book-sale-n09039.html.

3. Gary B. Nash. First City: Philadelphia and the Forging of Historical Memory (Philadelphia: University of Pennsylvania Press, 2002), pages 38–113. Also see Frank L. Mott. American Journalism: A History, 1690–1960 (New York: Macmillan, 1962), pages 404–405. Charles A. Madison. Book Publishing in America (New York: McGraw-Hill, 1966), page 132.

4. Tebbel. A History of Book Publishing in the United States, Vol. 1, The Creation of an Industry 1630–1865, pages 83, 91; Tebbel. A History of Book Publishing in the United States, Vol. 2, The Expansion of an Industry 1865–1919, pages 17–22, 185–186, 307–391; Tebbel. A History of Book Publishing in the United States, Vol. 3, The Golden Age between Two Wars, 1920–1940, pages 39–43; Tebbel A History of Book Publishing in the United States, Vol. 4, The Great Change, 1940–1980, pages 105–215; Tebbel. Between Covers: The Rise and Transformation of Book Publishing in America, pages 446–449, 462–466.

5. Michael E. Porter. "Clusters and the New Economics of Competition," Harvard Business Review 76, 6(November/December 1998): 77. Also see Richard Florida. "The Power of Density," The Atlantic, September 8, 2010, https://www.theatlantic.com/business/archive/2010/09/the-power-of-density/62569; Edwin McDowell. "For Publishing, The City, Remains 'The Mecca,'" The New York Times, March 15, 1983, https://www.nytimes.com/1983/03/15/nyregion/for-publishing-the-city-remains-the-mecca.html; Francisco Puig. "New Insights Regarding Clusters and Industrial Districts," Competitiveness Review: An International Business Journal, https://doi.org/10.1108/CR-03-2019-0033; Michael J. Weiss. The Clustered World: How We Live, What We Buy, and What It All Means About Who We Are (Boston: Little, Brown and Company2000), pages 36–38; Albert N. Greco. "Publishers in Migration." Publishers Weekly, October 12, 1992, pages 30–31; Tebbel. Between Covers: The Rise and Transformation of Book Publishing in America, 86–87, 171–172.

6. Some of the important societies and learned organizations in England in addition to the Royal Society include: the Royal Geographical Society. "Our

History;" https://www.rgs.org/about-us/our-history; Royal Society of Chemistry. "Our History;" https://www.rsc.org/about-us/our-history; British Science Association. " Our History; https://www.britishscienceas-sociation.org/Pages/Category/about.

7. The American Philosophical Society (APS). "About the APS;" https://www.amphilsoc.org/about.

8. The American Academy of Arts and Sciences (AAAS). "About Us;" https://www.amacad.org/abourt-academy.

9. U.S. Department of Labor (Labor), Bureau of Labor Statistics (BLS). "Historical Consumer Price Index for All Urban Consumers (CPI-U): U. S. City Average, All Items;" https://www.bls.gov/cpi/tables/historical-cpi-u-201710.pdf.

10. Cornell University Press. "About;" https://www.cornellpress.cornell.edu/about.

11. Johns Hopkins University Press. "About Hopkins Press;" https://www.press.jhu.edu/about-press.

12. Cecile M. Jagodzinski. "The University Press in North America: A Brief History," *Journal of Scholarly Publishing 40*, 1(October 2008): 2. Also see the Association of University Presses. "History of the Association;" https://aupresses.org/about-aupresses/history-of-the-association.

13. Dan Sinykin. *Big Fiction: How Conglomerates Changed the Publishing Industry and American Literature* (New York: Columbia University Press, 2023), page 195. Also see Boris Kachka. *Hot House: The Art of Survival of Art at America's Most Celebrated Publishing House Farrar, Straus & Giroux* (New York: Simon & Schuster; 2013), pages 266–292.

14. Al Silverman. *The Time of Their Lives: The Golden Age of Great American Publishers, Their Editors, and Authors*, page 2.

15. Jeffrey G. Williamson. "Globalization, Convergence, and History," *The Journal of Economic History 56*, 2(June 1996): 277–306. Also see Michael R. Czinkota and Ilkka A. Ronkainen. "The Globalization of the U.S. Economy: Consumer Market Implications," Journal of International Consumer Marketing; https://doi.org/10.1300/j046v03n04_05; 51–68. Kevin Stiroh. "Is There a New Economy?" https://doi.org/10.1080/05775132.1999.11472112; 82–101. Martin Albrow, John Eade, Neil Washbourne, and Jorg Durrschmidt. "The Impact of Globalization on Sociological Concepts: Community, Culture, and Milieu," https://doi.org/10.1080/13511610.1994.9968418; 371–389.

16. Oxford University Press. "Our Locations," https://jobs.oup.com/uk/jobs/ourlocations.

17. Ted Levitt. "Marketing Myopia," *Harvard Business Review*; https://hbr.org/2004/07/marketingmyopia.

18. Ibid.

19. Michael E. Porter. "The 5 Forces that Shape Strategy," *Harvard Business Review*; https://hbr.org/2008/01/the-5-forces-that-shape-strategy.

20. Albert N. Greco. *The Strategic Marketing of Science, Technology, and Medical Journals: A Business History of a Dynamic Marketplace 2000–2020* (Cham, Switzerland: Palgrave Macmillan, 2022), p. 38.

21. Tina E. Chrzastowski and Karen A. Schmidt. "The Serials Cancellation Crisis: National Trends in an Academic Library Serial Collections," *Library Acquisitions: Practice & Theory 21*, 4(Winter 1997): 431–443.

22. Emily R. Mobley. "Ruminations on the Sci-Tech Serials Crisis," Issues in Science and Technology Librarianship; https://doi.org/10.5062/f4v69gkr.

CHAPTER 3

Major Developments and Events in the Humanities and Scholarly Publishing: 2000–2014

Abstract A number of substantive trends in the humanities were evaluated, including undergraduate and graduate student enrollments, the number of college faculty members, humanities degrees and major humanities subjects, the impact of the "serials crisis," problems confronting academic libraries, journal trends and prices (including open access), and the number of scholarly books published by males and females. The results indicated that male academics published 2917 books (averaging 3.41 books) and the 760 female faculty members published 1918 books (averaging 2.52 books), indicating "gender disparity" in scholarly publishing.

Keywords Humanities degrees • Number of colleges • Open access • Publishing economics • Book prices • Journal prices • Serials crisis • Article processing charges (APCs) • Academic libraries • Consumer price index • Gender discrimination • Female book publishing • Male book publishing • Book title output • University presses • Commercial academic publishers

Number of U.S. Higher Education Students and Institutions

For decades, higher education students, faculty members, academic libraries, researchers, and general readers purchased humanities books. In the years 2000 to 2014, what were the substantive trends in these sectors?

A review of the statistical data from the U.S. Department of Education (Education) indicated that the number of higher education students increased significantly between 2000 and 2014. The number of undergraduates stood at 9,009,000 in 2000 and, by 2014, the tally grew an impressive +38.24% (topping 12,454,464). As for graduate students, including those working toward a master's degree or doctoral degrees, the totals were smaller than the undergraduates. In 2000, the total number of graduate students was 6,302,689, reaching 7,754,628 in 2014 (+23.04%).

A more detailed analysis revealed impressive annual percentage changes in both 2001–2002 and in 2008–2009. The recession of 2007–2009 eventually impacted negatively both undergraduate and graduate enrollments in the years 2011 to 2014.[1]

The total number of higher education institutions posted strong gains between 2001 (4182) and 2010 (4599) for an increase of +9.97%. These totals from Education include non-profit and for-profit higher education institutions. Ironically, the recession of 2007–2009 had no impact on the totals for 2011 (4707), 2012 (4726), and 2013 (4724). A -2.07% decrease was reported for 2014 (dropping to 4626). Table 3.1 has all of the details regarding the number of students and higher education institutions for 2000–2014.

In spite of the volatility of enrollments after 2010, the total number of higher education faculty members increased between 2001 and 2013. The majority of faculty members were employed full-time as either tenure track or tenured faculty. In 2001, that total was 618,000, and in 2013 it reached 791,000 (growing +27.99%). Part-time faculty members (often called contingent or adjunct faculty) worked on semester or year-long contracts, often at rather low pay per course(s) taught. In addition, these part-time faculty members rarely had access to medical, dental, vision care, or retirement opportunities. However, the part-time ranks grew +52.32% between

Table 3.1 Total U.S. non-profit public and private college students and colleges: 2000–2014

Year	Undergraduate and graduate students			Total annual percentage change	Total number of higher education institutions
	Full-time	Part-time	Total		
2000	9,009,600	6,302,689	15,312,289	–	4182
2001	9,447,502	6,480,485	15,927,987	+4.02%	4197
2002	9,946,359	6,665,352	16,611,711	+4.29%	4168
2003	10,326,133	6,585,348	16,911,481	+1.80%	4236
2004	10,610,177	6,661,867	17,272,044	+2.13%	4216
2005	10,797,011	6,690,464	17,487,475	+1.25%	4276
2006	10,957,536	6,796,692	17,754,230	+1.53%	4314
2007	11,270929	6,987,209	18,258,138	+2.84%	4352
2008	11,734636	7,347,050	19,081,686	+4.51%	4409
2009	12,605,355	7,708,239	20,313,594	+6.46%	4495
2010	13,087,182	7,932,256	21,019,438	+3.47%	4599
2011	13,002,531	8,008,059	21,010,590	-0.04%	4707
2012	12,734,404	7,910,074	20,644,478	-1.74%	4726
2013	12,596,610	7,780,067	20,376,677	-1.30%	4724
2014	12,454,464	7,754,628	20,209,092	-0.82%	4626
2000–2014 Percent change	+38.24 %	+23.04%	+31.98%	–	+10.62%

U.S. Department of Education. National Center for Education Statistics. *The Statistical Abstract of the U.S.*; various years. https://nces.ed.gov/programs/digest/d18/tables/dt18_303.10.asp
N.B. All numbers rounded off and may not always equal 100 percent. The totals for the number of colleges from Education and NCES included both non-profit and for-profit institutions

Table 3.2 Number of higher education faculty: 2001–2013

Year	Full-time	Part-time	Total
2001	618,000	495,000	1,113,000
2003	630,000	544,000	1,174,000
2005	676,000	615,000	1,290,000
2007	704,000	668,000	1,372,000
2009	729,000	710,000	1,439,000
2011	762,000	762,000	1,524,000
2013	791,000	754,000	1,545,000
2001–2013 Percent change	+27.99%	+52.32%	+38.81%

Source: *The Statistical Abstract of the United States*; various years
N.B. All totals rounded off and may not always equal 100%
Data not available for all years

2001 (495,000) and 2013 (754,000). Unfortunately, data for all years between 2000 and 2014 were not available. Table 3.2 has the details.

NUMBER OF PH.D. DEGREES: 2000–2014

The U.S. Department of Education (Education) released excellent datasets on the total number of Ph.D. degrees awarded in the United States. The constant growth in the number of Ph.D. degrees earned between 2000 (118,736) and 2014 (177,587) was a stunning +49.56%. This category did not experience any downward trends during those years, effectively escaping the ravages of the 2007–2009 recession that impacted employment in other sectors of the U.S. economy.

Looking at Ph.D. degrees in the humanities also revealed impressive, albeit a little uneven, annual growth rates. In 2000, 13,179 Ph.D. degrees were awarded in the humanities, accounting for 11.1% of all Ph.D. degrees. In 2014, the total stood at 15,450 (+17.23% between 2000 and 2014), although the share of humanities degrees as a percentage of all Ph.D. degrees fell to 8.7%. Table 3.3 has the details.

Drawing on data released by the U.S. Department of Education (Education), National Center for Education Statistics (NCES), and looking at the academic field of English language and literature, certainly one of the important humanities categories, the percentage of females earning a Ph.D. in that field exceeded significantly the number of males who earned that degree. For example, between 2000 and 2014, the percentage of female getting the Ph.D. never fell below the 58% mark, and, for several years, notably 2008, 2009, 2010, 2011, 2012, and 2014, the female percentage was in the 60% range. Table 3.4 has the details.

Since there are a large number of academic areas in the humanities, five important representative fields (with consistent annual data for 2000–2014) were selected for analysis, including area ethnic, cultural, and gender studies; communications, journalism, and related programs; English language and literature; foreign language and literature; and philosophy and religious studies. The area ethnic, cultural, and gender studies tallies for 2000 (305 Ph.D. degrees) and 2014 (336) were admirable, +63.90%. However, the eclectic communications, journalism, and related programs (which also included publishing studies) outpaced all of the five academic field with a +71.15% increase (2000; 357; 2014: 611).

While English language and literature was the largest of the five academic fields (with 18,460 Ph.D. degrees) between 2000 (1470) and 2014

Table 3.3 Total number of doctoral degrees awarded in the United States and in the humanities: 2000–2014

Year	Total number of all doctoral degrees	Percent of humanities' doctoral degrees	Total number of doctoral degrees in the humanities
2000	118,736	11.1	13,179
2001	119,585	10.8	12,915
2002	119,663	10.5	12,564
2003	121,579	10.1	12,279
2004	126,087	9.6	11,671
2005	134,387	8.9	11,960
2006	138,056	8.7	12,010
2007	144,690	7.9	11,430
2008	149,378	8.1	12,099
2009	154,425	8.4	12,971
2010	159,558	9.0	14,360
2011	163,827	9.4	15,399
2012	170,300	9.4	16,008
2013	175,026	9.3	16,277
2014	177,587	8.7	15,450
2000–2014			
Total	2,172,884		200,572
Average	144,858		13,371.47
Percent change 2000–2014	+49.56%		+17.23%

Source: U.S. Department of Education. National Center for Education Statistics; https://nces.ed.gov/propgrams/digest/d17/tables/dt17_318.20.asp; https://nces.ed.gov/programs/digest/d12/tables/dt12_310.asp; The American Academy of Arts and Sciences. "Humanities' Share of All Advanced [Doctoral] Degrees Conferred"; https://www.amacad.org/humanities-indicators/higher-education/humanities-share-all-advanced-degrees-conferred; *The Statistical Abstract of the United States*, various years

N.B. Excludes professional degrees
All numbers rounded off and may not always equal 100%. For data back to 1966, see Alvin B. Kernan, William G. Bowen, and Harold T. Shapiro (eds.). *What Happened to the Humanities?* (Princeton: Princeton University Press, 1997), p. 248

(1393), its total declined –5.24% during those years. This was, perhaps, an indicator of possible future results for this historically significant and large academic field. The last two categories posted smaller annual results. Foreign language and literature (with 16,604 Ph.D. degrees) recorded a +13.35% growth rate between 2000 (1086) and 2014 (1231). Philosophy and religious studies was the third largest Ph.D. field (with 9831

Table 3.4 Number of males and females earning the Ph.D. degree in English language and literature: 2000–2014

Year	Totals	Males	Females	Percent of total	
				Males	Females
2000	1470	611	859	41.56	58.44
2001	1330	533	797	40.08	59.92
2002	1291	532	759	41.21	58.79
2003	1246	492	754	39.49	60.51
2004	1207	479	728	36.69	60.31
2005	1212	494	718	40.76	59.24
2006	1254	510	744	40.35	58.86
2007	1178	478	700	40.58	59.42
2008	1262	453	809	35.90	64.10
2009	1271	464	807	36.51	63.49
2010	1334	523	811	39.21	60.79
2011	1344	529	815	39.36	60.64
2012	1427	548	879	38.40	61.60
2013	1377	554	823	40.23	59.77
2014	1393	557	836	39.99	60.01
2000–2014 Percent change	-5.24%	-8.84%	-2.68%	–	–

Source: U.S. Department of Education (Education), National Center for Education Statistics (NCES); https://nces.gov/pubs2016/2016014.pdf

Ph.D. degrees), growing +16.72% between 2000 (598) and 2014 (698). Table 3.5 has the details.

Number of Undergraduate and Graduate Degrees Awarded in the Humanities: 2000–2014

For some inexplicable reason, Education's academic fields for some undergraduate and master's degrees in the humanities differed somewhat from those used in the Ph.D. fields. Again, selecting four consistent and significant degree categories for undergraduate bachelor's degrees and master's degrees in the humanities revealed some substantive trends among the four categories selected. Two of the selected categories were English language and literature and foreign language and literature fields (i.e., these two categories were also used in the Ph.D. data in Table 3.4). However, the "philosophy and religious studies" Ph.D. category was split into two

Table 3.5 A selected number of doctoral degrees awarded in the humanities: 2000–2014

Year	Total number of humanities' doctorates in academic fields and sub-fields				
	Area ethnic, cultural & gender studies	Communications & journalism & related programs	English language & literature	Foreign language & literature	Philosophy & religious studies
2000	205	357	1470	1086	598
2001	216	368	1330	1078	612
2002	212	383	1291	1003	610
2003	186	398	1246	1042	662
2004	209	426	1207	1031	595
2005	189	468	1212	1027	586
2006	226	461	1254	1074	604
2007	233	479	1178	1059	637
2008	270	496	1262	1078	635
2009	239	533	1271	1111	686
2010	253	570	1334	1091	667
2011	278	577	1344	1158	667
2012	302	563	1427	1231	778
2013	291	612	1373	1304	796
2014	336	611	1393	1231	698
2000–2014 Total	3645	7302	18,460	16,604	9831
Percent change 2000–2014	+63.90%	+71.15%	−5.24%	+13.35%	+16.72%

Source: U.S. Department of Education, National Center for Education Statistics; https://nces.gov.edu/programs/digest/d17/tables/d17_318.20.asp.; https://nces.ed.gov/programs/digest/d21/tables/d21_318.20.asp; The Statistical Abstract of the United States; various years
N.B. The year "2011" refers to the academic year 2010–2011. "Communications & journalism & related programs" also refers to publishing studies. "History and the Social Sciences" were consolidated and were excluded
N.B. Totals not available for all years
All numbers rounded off and may not always equal 100%

undergraduate and graduate categories: philosophy and religious studies, and theology and religious vocations. These two were analyzed.

The total number of bachelor's degrees in English language and literature was immensely impressive, never falling below 50,000 between 2000 (when it recorded 50,106 degrees) and 2014 (50,464). For four years (2006: 55,096; 2007: 55,122; 2008: 55,038; and 2009: 55,462) the tally exceeded the 55,000 mark. Overall, this academic field increased a very modest +0.71% between 2000 and 2014, impacted perhaps by concerns about either total graduate school costs (e.g., tuition, room and board, and educational materials) and/or higher education job placement opportunities.

Foreign language and literature, while smaller than English language and literature, recorded a growth rate of +22.71%, and for seven continuous years (between 2007 and 2013), it posted strong results in the +20,000 range. The philosophy and religious studies field outpaced the annual percentage changes for both the English and foreign language and literature fields with a strong +29.72%. For 11 straight years (2004–2014), its tally never went below 11,000, for 5 years it was in the +12,000 range (2008, 2009, 2010, 2012, 2013), and one year (2011) exceeded the 14,000 mark. Theology and religious vocations was the smallest of the four bachelor's degrees categories; however, its +43.00% annual growth

Table 3.6   A selected number of humanities bachelor's degrees: 2000–2014

Year	English language and literature	Foreign language and literature and linguistics	Philosophy and religious studies	Theology and religious vocations
2000	50,106	15,886	8535	6789
2001	50,569	16,128	9442	6220
2002	52,375	16,258	9473	7762
2003	53,670	16,901	10,344	7926
2004	53,984	17,754	11,152	8126
2005	54,379	18,386	11,584	9244
2006	55,096	19,410	11,985	8548
2007	55,122	20,275	11,969	8696
2008	55,038	20,977	12,257	8992
2009	55,462	21,158	12,444	8940
2010	53,229	21,507	12,503	8719
2011	52,754	21,708	14,336	7567
2012	53,765	21,756	12,645	9304
2013	52,401	21,647	12,792	9385
2014	50,464	19,493	11,072	9708
2000–2014 Percent change	+0.71%	+22.71%	+29.72%	+43.00%

Source: *The Statistical Abstract of the United States*, various years. N.B. History data was combined with the social sciences. All numbers rounded off. For data back to 1966, see Alvin B. Kernan, William G. Bowen, and Harold T. Shapiro (eds.). *What Happened to the Humanities?* (Princeton: Princeton University Press, 1997), p. 249

rate was exceptionally impressive, growing from 6789 in 2000 to 9708 in 2014. Table 3.6 has all of the data for these four fields.

Using the same four academic humanities categories for master's degrees for 2000–2014 revealed small totals but very impressive growth rates. English language and literature increased +32.10% with seven years (2008 through 2014) in the +9000 range. Foreign language and literature was smaller than English (2000: 3407; 2014: 3482) with a +2.20% annual growth rate. Philosophy and religious studies was also a small category with 1376 degrees in 2000 and 2095 in 2014. However, it generated a superior +52.25% annual growth rate between 2000–2014. The theology and religious vocation academic category emerged as a growth field. In 2000, it awarded 5534 degrees, growing to 14,128 in 2024, +155.29% (the largest annual growth rate of any undergraduate or graduate category in the humanities). It is possible that many of the individuals earning a

Table 3.7   A selected number of humanities master's degrees: 2000–2014

Year	English language and literature	Foreign language and literature and linguistics	Philosophy and religious studies	Theology and religious vocations
2000	7022	3407	1376	5534
2001	6763	3035	1534	9728
2002	7097	3075	1371	4909
2003	7413	3049	1578	5099
2004	7956	3124	1578	5486
2005	8468	3407	1647	5815
2006	8845	3539	1739	6092
2007	8742	3443	1716	6446
2008	9161	3565	1879	6996
2009	9261	3592	1859	12,836
2010	9201	3755	2043	12,824
2011	9475	3727	2257	12,752
2012	9939	3827	2003	13,396
2013	9755	3708	1931	14,276
2014	9292	3482	2095	14,128
2000–2014 Percent	+32.10%	+2.20%	+52.25%	+155.29%

Source: *The Statistical Abstract of the United States*, various years
N.B. Data for history was combined with the social sciences
All numbers rounded off

master's degree in this category were either members of a religious organization or studying for a religious career. Table 3.7 has the details.

New Academic Book Title Output: 2000–2014

The majority of academics (as well as researchers at various organizations and libraries) work and live in a publish or perish environment. So, publishing a book enables an academic or a librarian to get hired, tenured, and promoted. University presses, societies, and commercial scholarly publishers realized that scholarly academic books in the humanities have long played the preeminent pathway (often called the "gold standard") to success in higher education in the United States. With the growth in the total number of higher education faculty members between 2001 and 2013 (+38.81%), increase in the total number of Ph.D. degrees awarded between 2000 and 2014 (+49.56%), and in the humanities (+17.23%), it would be reasonable to assume that the percentage increase in the total number of new academic books (both hardcover and paperback) would be "similar" to the percentage increases of faculty members and Ph.D. degrees during those years.

However, that reasonable assumption was wrong. It appears that the publish or perish policy triggered an overwhelmingly large increase in new title output, topping +99.39% between 2000 and 2014. Looking at the years 2000–2006, new titles hovered in the upper 60,000 and lower 70,000 range. In 2007, title output jumped to 93,082. The recession of 2007–2009 apparently had no impact on the number of new books published, reaching 106,810 in 2008 and 107,753 in 2009. By 2011 the total reached a staggering 120,482, then posting an even higher tally of 138,895 in 2014. Overall, 1,403,919 new academic books were published between 2000 and 2014, +99.39%, averaging 93,594.60 books each year. Table 3.8 has the annual totals.

These are very large totals. It is difficult to understand how the number of academics, higher education and research libraries, students, or general readers in the United States, or sales in the important and growing global market for books in the humanities, could absorb this almost unfettered outpouring of scholarly books about, for example, Jane Austen, Nietzsche, F. Scott Fitzgerald, Toni Morison, Martin Luther, or Franklin D. Roosevelt.

However, the basic problem academics faced was to get published by an important university or a commercial scholarly publisher press (and many of them were "ranked" on various websites). The first book was often a

Table 3.8 Total new academic book title output: 2000–2014

Year	New title output
2000	69,157
2001	70,572
2002	72,169
2003	63,509
2004	60,111
2005	75,384
2006	77,534
2007	93,082
2008	106,810
2009	107,753
2010	107,802
2011	120,482
2012	120,837
2013	120,822
2014	137,895
2005–2014	
Total	1,403,919
Percent change	+99.39%

Source: American Library Association

revision of the Ph.D. dissertation, which received generally a substantial amount of publishing support from the Ph.D. advisor to individuals that the senior researcher knew in the scholarly publishing community. While this initial introduction to the scholarly publishing world was often fraught with tension and uncertainty, the academic then faced the next more difficult hurdle to achieve tenure and promotion: the elusive "second" scholarly book. Danielle A. Macdonald and Laura M. Stevens remarked that

> faculty careers stall at the associate professor rank for all sorts of complicated reasons. But one professional hurdle impedes promotions more than any other: the second book. Despite the widely publicized pressures on academic libraries and [scholarly] presses, books remain as important as ever for career advancement and scholarly impact. In most of the humanities and some of the social sciences, the publication of a second book is the central accomplishment that faculty members, especially at research-oriented institutions, must show to earn promotion to full or even associate professors [at some elite universities].[2]

So how difficult was it for a faculty member to get a first and then a second book published by a university press or a commercial academic press? A related and clearly a pivotal question centered on the question of diversity. Was it more difficult for a female academic to get published?

In an article by Nicole Benevento, et al.,[3] the researchers analyzed the number of scholarly books (excluding textbooks) published between 2000 and 2014 by university presses and commercial scholarly publishers by 1633 academics (873 males, 53.46% of the total; and 760 females, 46.54%) at the "top fifty" English departments in the United States (as determined by *U.S. News*). It is likely that scholarly books released by societies were "comingled" with the university press data by *U.S. News* as well as by Education. Their results indicated that, during the years 2000–2014, 873 male academics published 2917 books (averaging 3.41 books for each male faculty member). As for the 760 female faculty members, they had 1918 books (averaging 2.52 books). So, these academics published a total of 4835 scholarly books; male academics responsible for 60.33% of that total, with females accounted for 39.67%.

When the datasets were divided by Benevento, et al., into the top ten ranked English departments and the bottom ten, the results were again dominated by males: top ten, 671 books, averaging 3.83 books; and the bottom ten: 361 books, 2.65 average. As for female faculty members: in the top ten departments: 471 books, averaging 3.16; in the bottom ten: 262 books, 2.50 average. Looking at the top ten departments, academics published a total of 1032 books; and males accounted for 65.02% with females at 45.64%. In the bottom ten (for a total of 623 books), males published 57.95% of that total with females at 42.05%.[4]

So, looking at the results in the NCES datasets and the Benevento, et al. study there were more females earning the Ph.D. than males between 2000 and 2014: there were slightly more male faculty members (873; 53.46%) than female academics (760; 46.54%); and fewer books were published by female authors overall, in the top 50 departments, the top ten, and in the bottom ten English departments.[5] Clearly, there appears to be substantive statistical data about gender disparity in the publication output of female academics between 2000 and 2014 in the top 50 English language and literature departments in the United States.

A Selected List of Academic Books in the Humanities: Number of Titles and Average Prices: 2000–2014

While Education was not consistent in its categorization of academic degrees, the U.S. book industry utilized standard book categories.[6] However, it was important to select academic book categories (for both new titles and average prices) that corresponded basically to the major degree categories in the humanities. So, four book categories were selected for analysis, including fine and applied arts, history, language and literature (which included both English and foreign), and philosophy and religion.

In the fine and applied arts category, new title output increased +96.24%, growing from 3853 in 2000 to 7561 new titles in 2014. Overall, there were 86,886 new titles released in this category between 2000 and 2014, averaging annually 5,792.40, and prices surged +45.26% (increasing from an average of $46.07 in 2000 to $66.92 in 2014.

History (i.e., all periods from ancient to late modern to current years) remained a large and important category posting strong results in new titles between 2000 and 2014 (+75.62%). Totals topped 135,925 with an average annual output of 9065.00. Prices for books in this category remained high during those years, growing from $43.03 in 2000 to $70.61 in 2014 (+44.09%). The diversified language and literature category generated the largest number of new titles (260,448; +132.12%) in the four categories under analysis with annual averages of 17,363.20. However, these books were not the most expensive ones among the four categories increasing from $36.90 in 2000 to only $57.90 in 2014 (+56.91%).

Philosophy and religion books, on the other hand, generated the largest price point increases increasing from $44.84 in 2000 to $87.32 in 2014 (+94.74%). These tallies were impacted by the release of 101,863 new titles (2000: 4961; 2014: 10,564). The annual average output was 6790.87. Table 3.9 has the details for all four book categories.

Traditionally, academic books were sold in a variety of bookstores, ranging from small independents (called "indies") to large chain bookstores often located in malls (e.g., Barnes & Noble, B & N; Borders; Books-a-Million) to college bookstores managed generally by the higher

Table 3.9 Academic book title output (units) and average prices: 2000–2014 (U.S. dollars)

Year	Fine & applied arts		History		Language & literature		Philosophy & religion	
	Titles	Prices	Titles	Prices	Titles	Prices	Titles	Prices
2000	3853	$46.07	7046	$43.03	11,655	$36.90	4961	$44.84
2001	5116	$51.11	7151	$39.46	12,189	$34.07	4631	$44.09
2002	5274	$58.19	7771	$40.68	12,645	$35.83	5091	$45.02
2003	4839	$58.61	7967	$42.04	15,695	$32.46	5230	$46.12
2004	3728	$48.41	7811	$43.26	15,242	$33.93	5026	$48.63
2005	4215	$48.16	7174	$49.47	12,391	$41.53	5636	$53.31
2006	4652	$52.77	7296	$52.54	12,551	$45.69	5745	$59.32
2007	6573	$49.95	8531	$54.48	17,351	$41.53	6626	$59.18
2008	6767	$54.17	10,380	$59.10	18,368	$45.69	7522	$65.79
2009	6647	$54.07	10,415	$55.98	19,707	$48.32	7574	$67.91
2010	5538	$57.17	11,179	$66.29	19,364	$57.31	7686	$81.75
2011	7866	$63.68	10,729	$74.99	21,247	$60.21	8706	$88.74
2012	7098	$66.76	9857	$73.31	21,813	$61.12	8473	$84.73
2013	7159	$68.24	10,293	$75.82	23,176	$59.32	8392	$97.38
2014	7561	$66.92	12,375	$70.61	27,054	$57.9	10,564	$87.32
2000–2014 Percent change	+96.24%	+45.26%	+75.62%	+64.09%	+132.12%	+56.91%	+112.94%	+94.74%

Source: American Library Association

N.B. These are average prices; these totals do not include any discounts offered by publishers and/or distributors

All numbers rounded off

education bookstore chains (B & N Education, Follett) or, in some instances, managed by the college or by local independent bookstores.[7]

The total number of bookstores in the United States grew sharply between 1980 (17,218) and 1995 (28,510, +65.58%). However, various online sites selling academic and other books (new, rentals, used) emerged challenging the strong market position held by the indies, the mall-operated chains, or the college bookstore. The tide turned precipitously with the launch of an obscure online operation in Seattle. Amazon.com was launched on July 16, 1995. This event, and the proliferation of other online websites, triggered a downward spiral that engulfed the once strong traditional bookstore environment, which experienced a -19.11% decline between 1980 and 2014 with an even sharper drop of -51.15% between 1995 and 2014.

Clearly, this metamorphosis impacted scholarly publishers. The online sites, including those operated and maintained by publishers in a direct-to-consumer sale, offered publishers and authors access to more potential readers and buyers of their humanities books in the United States and abroad. However, the university presses, societies, and commercial academic publishers had to cope with new requests or requirements from the online sites for larger discount rates (called "points" or "discount points" in the publishing world) than the traditional discounts utilized in the indie or chain or college bookstore sector. In addition, these publishers had to comply with more complicated shipping and returns policies. In reality, the internet created almost endless opportunities to showcase a book, and it was also a "disruptive" technology that rattled the foundations of what had been a rather staid publishing business.[8] Table 3.10 has the details about the number of bookstore and their revenues between 1980 and 2014.

THE PRICE OF SERIALS IN THE HUMANITIES: 2000–2014

While books remained the "gold standard" in the humanities, many academics, graduate students, and librarians also published articles (and especially in certain journals in literature and history) and book reviews in the growing number of scholarly journals in the humanities. Regrettably, the primary serials categories differed somewhat from the traditional book categories employed in the United States. Five scholarly journal categories in the humanities were selected for analysis that were "similar" to the book categories, including arts and architecture, history, language and literature

Table 3.10 U.S. bookstores: 1980–2014 and bookstore annual revenues: 1980–2014 ($ billions)

Year	Total number of bookstores	Annual bookstore revenues
1980	17,218	$2.59
1981	17,709	$2.99
1982	19,049	$3.27
1983	19,580	$3.75
1984	21,528	$4.12
1985	21,612	$4.45
1986	21,568	$4.76
1987	21,819	$5.34
1988	22,926	$6.00
1989	24,319	$6.54
1990	22,928	$7.43
1991	24,854	$7.73
1992	26,787	$8.33
1993	27,809	$9.11
1994	28,137	$10.11
1995	28,510	$11.20
1996	28,280	$11.91
1997	27,691	$12.74
1998	27,930	$13.28
1999	25,130	$14.17
2000	25,921	$14.88
2001	25,916	$15.10
2002	25,137	$15.44
2003	22,321	$16.22
2004	23,643	$16.88
2005	20,677	$16.99
2006	19,321	$16.98
2007	18,456	$17.17
2008	18,064	$16.80
2009	17,312	$15.80
2010	16,968	$15.24
2011	15,533	$13.72
2012	14,939	$12.27
2013	14,567	$11.45
2014	13,928	$11.25
1980–2014 Percent change	-19.11%	+334.36%
1995–2014 Percent change	-51.15%	2007–2014 -34.48%

Source: *The Bowker Annual* and the *Library and Book Trade Almanac*; various years. U.S. Department of Commerce, Bureau of the Census. https://www.census.gov/retail/index.html. U.S. Department of Commerce, Bureau of the Census. https://www.census.gov/retail/index.html

N.B.: The total number of bookstores includes the total number of chain and independent bookstores selling new and used books

All numbers rounded off and may not always equal 100%. In the United States, "bookstores" include a wide variety of retail establishments, including antiquarian, chains, college, independents, religious, used, etc. Bookstore totals were not available for all years (which also combined both English and foreign language and literature), music (i.e., music history), and all of the various themes, histories, and schools in philosophy and religion. While all five categories posted strong annual price increases between 2000 and 2014, the annual paid subscription prices for all of them were significantly lower than the ones in the high profile, highly cited science, technology, and medicine (STM) journals.[9]

For example, in 2014 the average paid subscription price (by a research or university library or an individual) for arts and architecture journals was $290; the other ones in the humanities in that same year included history, $303; language and literature, $231; music, $307; and philosophy and religion, $307. For example, some of the STM journal annual subscription

Table 3.11   Average price of humanities serials: 2000–2014 (U.S. dollars)

Year	Arts & architecture	History	Language & literature	Music	Philosophy & religion
2000	$121.00	$116.00	$102.00	$87.00	$136.00
2001	$127.00	$123.00	$111.00	$91.00	$145.00
2002	$134.00	$132.00	$120.00	$96.00	$156.00
2003	$144.00	$152.00	$135.00	$105.00	$174.00
2004	$160.00	$171.00	$153.00	$110.00	$195.00
2005	$172.00	$189.00	$166.00	$127.00	$211.00
2006	$185.00	$201.00	$176.00	$130.00	$226.00
2007	$245.00	$202.00	$203.00	$151.00	$240.00
2008	$272.00	$226.00	$223.00	$198.00	$262.00
2009	$236.00	$262.00	$236.00	$182.00	$270.00
2010	$263.00	$282.00	$256.00	$217.00	$286.00
2011	$281.00	$300.00	$270.00	$222.00	$306.00
2012	$296.00	$318.00	$286.00	$233.00	$325.00
2013	$331.00	$284.00	$302.00	$180.00	$264.00
2014	$290.00	$308.00	$303.00	$231.00	$307.00
2000–2014 Percent change	+139.67%	+165.52%	+197.06%	+165.52%	+125.74%

Source: American Library Association
N.B. These are average prices; these totals do not include any discounts offered by publishers and/or distributors
All numbers rounded off

prices included biology, $2081; chemistry, $3708; geology, $1390; mathematics, $1251; and physics, $3083.[10]

These STM journal prices triggered intense discussions and debates in the United States, but mainly in certain foreign markets (e.g., Canada and Europe), about the increasing cost of journals. This became known as the "serials crisis," and it generated a series of major articles, pronouncements, and guidelines to create and maintain (and in some instances to mandate) "open access" (OA) policies for scholarly journals. Table 3.11 has the totals for the humanities journals.

THE IMPACT OF TECHNOLOGY AND THE "SERIALS CRISIS" ON SCHOLARLY PUBLISHING

After 2000, computers (i.e., traditional desk computers, laptops, and tablets) became ubiquitous at colleges and universities. As computer prices began slowly to become more reasonable, memory and speed increased rapidly.[11] In addition, the emergence and wide acceptance of smart phones,[12] "Zoom" type video and audio systems,[13] and social media platforms[14] also impacted directly how academics and students accessed scholarly information and communicated and worked with individuals, especially at other universities.

These new "disruptive" but widely adopted and utilized technologies, along with increases in the annual paid journal subscription costs by libraries and individuals, sparked intense debates that many academics (at small colleges in the United States and especially in "developing" nations with limited library resources and budgets) did not have access to important scholarly articles. This belief, about scholarly journals and articles locked behind subscription pay walls, triggered serious discussions in the United States, Canada, and especially in Europe, about the possibility of employing computer technologies to either lower subscription costs (by reducing certain expenses and procedures) and/or to create new, innovative computer systems able to provide free, digital, open access (OA) scholarly literature to any academic or student in the world. In essence, journals and articles would be free.

So, a number of editors and publishers of scholarly journals, some before 2000 and more after 2000, began to move away from paid journal subscriptions and adopted various options. First, some OA journals adopted what has been called a "hybrid" system. That is, a researcher had the option to convey the article's copyright to the publisher and the journal article would be available only to libraries or individuals who had a paid subscription to the journal. A second option was for the author (or in reality the author's funding agency) to pay a fee to the journal (called an article processing charges; APC), keep the copyright, and allow the journal to make the article free to any library or reader in the world (generally under a Creative Commons CC-By license).

Another possibility was a journal could go completely OA (known as a "gold" open access option), charge the author(s) an APC, and make the article and indeed the entire issue of a journal free to everyone. Some examples of the movement toward OA humanities journals included the well-known *Journal of Eastern Mediterranean Archaeology and Heritage Studies*[15] and the *Tulsa Studies in Women's Literature*.[16]

OA needed a clearly defined definition and theoretical foundation to convince the academic community that the movement toward OA would benefit the entire university and research sectors. Peter Suber, at Harvard University, emerged as one of the early and influential proponents of the OA movement in the United States. In an important article, originally published on December 29, 2004, Suber defined OA as

> Open-access (OA) literature is digital, online, free of charge, and free of most copyright and licensing restrictions... In most fields, scholarly journals do not pay authors, who can therefore consent to OA without losing revenue... OA literature is not free to produce, even if it is less expensive to produce than conventionally published literature. The question is not whether scholarly literature can be made costless, but whether there are better ways to pay the bills than by charging readers and creating access barriers. Business models for paying the bills depend on how OA is delivered.[17]

Suber provided two possible OA models. First, academics could create OA archives or OA repositories. Second, OA journals could "perform peer review, and then make the approved contents freely available to the world."[18] Suber's OA ideas spread, and he eventually wrote an OA book for MIT Press in 2012 that was freely available to anyone.[19] In addition to opening up the scholarly journal pay wall, it was argued that a researcher's article, perhaps a new interpretation about the British poets Lord Bryon, Percy Bysshe Shelley, John Keats, William Wordsworth, and Samuel Taylor Coleridge would be seen and read by more scholars. This meant effectively increasing the importance of the research, and the author, inside and outside the academic community.

In essence, the many proponents of OA, which included librarians and academics, believed that an author working at a government-funded university or a research center and/or receiving a research grant from a governmental agency (perhaps the Department of Agriculture, DOA; or the National Institutes of Health, NIH) had the funds (from the university or in the research grant) available to pay an APC. In reality, this assumption made great sense if one viewed only the science, technology, and medicine (STM) scholarly publishing sector and academics at government-funded colleges and universities.[20]

DID NEWTON PROVIDE THE ANSWER TO APCs?

If a journal decided to become a "hybrid" or a complete OA journal (sometimes called a "gold" OA journal), it had to cover its costs. While some individuals maintained that the editors, associate and assistant editors, and members of the editorial board provided free labor, which enabled the journal to reap tremendous profits, in reality the concept that journal articles would be free was at best based on a complete lack of any understanding about the economics of publishing. One Princeton University librarian writing in the *Academic Librarian* reported that "librarians have been cutting serials and complaining about [scholarly journal] vendors for a generation at least, and working diligently to educate academics about the economics of scholarly communications...[But academics] have every incentive to keep publishing in the top journals and no incentive to publish only in open access journals."[21]

Sir Isaac Newton was concerned about physics and not journal publishing costs; however, his First Law of Motion described what happened when APCs were introduced into academia. Newton's First Law of Motion "states that a body at rest will remain at rest unless an outside force acts on it; and a body in motion at a constant velocity will remain in motion in a straight line unless acted upon by an outside force."[22]

Since the first scholarly journal was published in January 1665, there was stability in the scholarly journal world; in essence the journal world was at "rest" because scholarly journals were paid subscription journals and/or provided to the members of an academic society because of a paid membership fee. When an unbalancing force (i.e., OAs and APCs) were introduced into the scholarly publishing world, the traditional "balance" (i.e., the well-established paid subscription business model) was upended.

Table 3.12 Profit and loss (P & L) elements for a scholarly journal published by a university press or a society: 2014

A printed journal	*A digital-only journal*
Editorial costs	**Editorial costs**
Editor's annual fee	Editor's annual fee
Associate/assistant editor's annual fee	Associate/assistant editor's annual fee
Office expenses	Office expenses
Annual conference expenses	Annual conference expenses
Tracking article submissions	Tracking article submissions
Assigning peer reviewers	Assigning peer reviewers
Handling peer reviews and resubmits	Handling peer reviews and resubmits
Computer plagiarism review	Computer plagiarism review
Cross referencing article review	Cross referencing article review
Technical review of articles	Technical review of articles
Copyediting	Copyediting
Total:	Total:
Production Costs	**Production Costs**
Plant (editorial, art, design, page make-up)	Plant (editorial, art, design, page make-up)
Printing, paper, & binding (PPB) (Number of copies, illustrations, etc.)	N/A
Warehousing	Computer "warehousing" and maintenance
Mail distribution	Computer distribution
Handling returned copies	N/A
Total:	Total:
Revenues	
Number of paid subscriptions	Number of paid subscriptions
Different subscription rates:	Different subscription rates:
Domestic, international	Domestic, international
Libraries, individuals	Libraries, individuals
Advertising	Advertising
Article reprints	Article reprints
Misc.	Misc.
Total:	Total:
Overhead	**Overhead**
Employee pay & benefits	Employee pay & benefits
Taxes: N/A	Taxes: N/A
Marketing	Marketing
Legal expenses	Legal expenses
Insurance	Insurance

(*continued*)

Table 3.12 (continued)

A printed journal	A digital-only journal
Telephone & FAX	Telephone & FAX
Email	Email
Computer equipment & technology	Computer equipment & technology
Inventory write-off	Inventory write-off
Office rent	Office rent
Misc.	Misc.
Total:	Total:
Total Revenues:	**Total Revenues:**
Minus total costs:	Minus total costs:
Minus overhead expenses:	Minus overhead expenses
Net revenue:	Net revenue:

Suber realized that someone has to pay to make a journal or a journal article free, even a digital one; and a large percentage of the scholarly journal publishers at university presses, academic societies, and commercial scholarly publishers also realized this rather basic economic principle. In reality, scholarly publishers had to understand and cope with the five basic economic principles that impacted every publisher and every consumer of research. They include scarcity, the law of supply and demand, marginal costs, marginal benefits, and incentives. Clearly, every publisher of a journal had fixed and variable expenses and costs as well as revenues (which can be somewhat erratic at times due to the impact of recessions or the number of paid subscribers). Table 3.12 lists these basic expense items for both a printed and a digital journal, and many costs do not disappear in an all-digital OA world. It appears that most academics wanted and needed to get published, and very few were interested, as the author at the *Academic Librarian* pointed out, in either understanding or addressing the fundamental economics of publishing.

OA and APCs allowed journal publishers to generate the revenues they needed to cover their myriad costs and expenses. Heather Morrison, Jihane Salhab, Alexis Calve-Genest, and Tony Horava analyzed the 9702 OA journals and APCs that were listed, as of May 15, 2014, in the comprehensive Directory of Open Access Journals (DOAJ). Of that total, 6470 (67%) did not have APCs. However, 2567 (26%) charged APCs, and an additional 520 (5%) had "conditional charges." There was no information about the remaining 145 journals (1%).[23] APCs ranged from no cost to a high of $4114, and the average APC was $964.[24] The average APC for a university press was $744; it was $1295 for a commercial scholarly published journal and $1562 for a society.[25]

Richard Van Noorden, writing in *Nature*, commented on the acceptance of OA journals, especially in the STM fields. "By 2011, 11% of the world's [STM] journal articles were being published in fully open access journals."[26] Van Noorden's analyses of OA prices corresponded to the research of Morrison, et al. "The largest open access publisher—BioMed-Central and PloS—charge $1,350 to $2,250 to publish peer-reviewed articles in many of their journals."[27]

Peter Suber revisited OA concerns in an important 2013 article in *The Guardian*. Suber was concerned about generally accepted "myths" (especially economic issues and mandated policies, especially in Europe or by the U.S. government) that he believed had undermined the movement toward OA. He insisted that academics, more or less, understood OA journals. "I say 'more or less' because the common misunderstanding of open access journals is itself myth-ridden... By contrast repositories [i.e., pre-print repositories of scholarly journals] are comparatively new in the scholarly landscape, making them easy to overlook."[28] Suber also maintained that OA mandates "infringe academic freedom. This is true for gold access but not for green [i.e., articles placed on a repository maintained by an academic, an academic department, or a university]."[29]

ACADEMIC LIBRARIES CONFRONT THE SERIALS CRISIS

The U.S. Department of Education (Education), National Center for Education Statistics (NCES) released some datasets for a selected number of years (i.e., 2004, 2006, 2008, 2010, and 2012) about college libraries (ranging from 3653 in 2004 to 3793 in 2012). In essence, they listed the vast majority of the non-profit higher education institutions in the United States during those years and their total library expenditures (which included salaries, utilities, book purchases, etc.) as well as expenditures for serials and digital serials. Total library expenditures increased +21.8% between 2004 and 2012. Serials expenditures jumped +41.08% during those years; however, the costs for digital serials skyrocketed +199.22%. Table 3.13 has the details.

However, the serials crisis impacted higher education libraries in a myriad of other ways. First, all library expenditures as a percentage of college budgets declined sharply for a number of years. For example, in 1984, the

Table 3.13   Academic library number of volumes and expenditures: 2004–2012

Year	Number of libraries	Total library expenditures	Total serials expenditures	
			Total	Digital
2004	3653	$5,751,247,194	$1,363,671,792	$480,137,504
2006	3617	$6,234,191,836	$1,521,721,559	$691,584,934
2008	3827	$6,785,542,230	$1,704,298,887	$1,004,393,298
2010	3689	$6,829,108,368	$1,786,083,064	$1,249,726,269
2012	3793	$7,008,113,939	$1,923,935,307	$1,436,670,505
Percent change 2004–2012	+3.83%	+21.85%	+41.08%	+199.22%

Source: U.S. Department of Education (Education). National Center for Education Statistics (NCES); https://nces.ed.gov/surveys/libraries

Table 3.14 U.S. college library expenditures as a percentage of total university expenditures: 1984–2011

Year	Percentage
1984	3.70%
1987	3.50%
1989	3.30%
1992	3.10%
1997	2.90%
2000	2.90%
2001	2.80%
2002	2.48%
2003	2.31%
2004	2.40%
2005	2.30%
2006	2.20%
2007	2.20%
2008	2.10%
2009	2.00%
2010	1.93%
2011	1.80%

Source: Phil Davis. "Libraries Receive Shrinking Share of University Expenditures; https://scholarlykitchen.sspnet.org/2014/07/22/libraries-receive-shrinking-share
N.B. Data not available for all years

Table 3.15 The
U.S. Consumer Price
Index (CPI):
2000–2014

Year	Annual average CPI:	Annual percent change
	All urban consumers	Rate of inflation
2000	172.2	3.4%
2001	177.1	2.8%
2002	179.9	1.6%
2003	184.0	2.3%
2004	188.9	2.7%
2005	195.3	3.4%
2006	201.6	3.2%
2007	207.3	2.9%
2008	215.3	3.8%
2009	214.5	-0.4%
2010	218.1	1.6%
2011	224.9	3.2%
2012	229.6	2.1%
2013	233.0	1.5%
2014	236.7	1.6%

Source: Federal Reserve Bank Minneapolis; https://www.min-neapolisfed.org/abouit-us/monetary-policy/inflation-calculator/consumer-price-index-1913

percentage was 3.70%. By 1992 it was reduced to 3.10%, and it continued to decline at an alarming rate reaching 2.90% in 2000, 2.3% in 2005, and only 1.80% in 2011. Table 3.14 has the details.

Second, the nation experienced a surge in the Consumer Price Index (CPI) between 2000 and 2014, jumping +37.46%. Table 3.15 has the details. The CPI total exceeded the annual increase in higher education's library expenditures as well as the growth in the cost of humanities books (see Table 3.9) and humanities journals (see Table 3.11). Third, the cost to maintain a scholarly book on a college library shelf was $4.26 per book in 2014, and, if a book were stored on an off-site facility, the cost per title was 86 cents.

Fourth, certain universities had the resources to fund more adequately library expenditures. For example, during the 2012–2013 academic year, Harvard University's total library expenditures was $117,316,662 and Yale's total was $84,665,297.[30] However, these institutions were the exception. The University of Florida's 2014–2015 library budget, a major university in the South, was $7,069,810.[31] In 2014, Rutgers University

Table 3.16 Annual revenues for major commercial scholarly publishers and university presses: 2009–2014 (U.S. dollars in millions)

Year	RELX	Wolters Kluwer	John Wiley	Springer	Informa	Oxford University Press	Cambridge University Press
2009	$7756	$4910	$1611	$1228	$1074	$938	N/A
2010	$7149	$4719	$1699	$1149	$1039	$941	N/A
2011	$5686	$4360	$1743	$1138	$1069	$1104	N/A
2012	$5934	$4766	$1783	$1298	$1126	$1125	$396
2013	$6093	$4920	$1761	$1301	$1185	$1254	$433
2014	$5362	$4455	$1822	$1167	$1075	$1181	$409

Source: *Publishers Weekly* (*PW*); various issues
N.B. Data not available for years before 2009 and for Cambridge University Press for the years 2009, 2010, and 2011
PW rounded off all numbers

(in N.J.) cut its library budget by $550,000.[32] The American Library Association (ALA) reported that "just over half of academic libraries, 2,023 had total expenditures of less than $500,000 in fiscal year 2012."[33] *American Libraries Magazine* addressed college closures or the termination of degrees. "When a university cuts majors, programs, or even an entire school, what happens to its library? The obvious answer: nothing good."[34]

Fifth, many critics of the serials crisis, as well as increase in the price of scholarly books, blamed the commercial scholarly publishers for raising the price of serials and books. However, a review of financial data from *Publishers Weekly* revealed the fact that, while the commercial publishers did generate impressive annual revenues, they also had to cope with changes in the CPI. In fact, two of these publishers posted declines in revenues between 2009 and 2014, and one was essentially flat during those years. Table 3.16 has the details.

CONCLUSION

Individuals, colleges, libraries, and scholarly publishers experienced the impact of an increase in inflation while trying to cope with the costs of normal annual expenditures. Clearly, the years 2000–2014 were difficult ones for publishers, college administrators, and librarians. However, the events after 2014 tested the mettle of the entire academic publishing ecosystem.

NOTES

1. National Bureau of Economic Research (NBER). "U.S. Business Cycle Expansions and Contractions;" https://www.nber.org/research/data/us-business-ccycle-expansions-and-contractions.
2. Danielle A. Macdonald and Laura M. Stevens. "Associate Professors and the 'Second Book Problem';" https://www.chronicle.com/article/associate-professor-and-the-second-book-problem.
3. Nicole Benvento, Albert N. Greco, Toniann Pasqueralle, Clara Rodriguez, Francesca Russo, Alana M. Spendley, Kelly Sullivan, Yiming Sun, and Robert M. Wharton. "Who Publishes More Books in U.S. English Departments, Men or Women?" *Publishing Research Quarterly*; https://doi.org/10.1007/s121109-017-9548-x.
4. Ibid. Also see Modern Language Association (MLA). MLA Office of Research: 2010; https://www.mla.org/center/download/3208/81186/sed_0708.pdf.
5. Albert N. Greco. *The Economics of the Publishing and Information Industries: the Search for Yield in a Disintermediated* World (New York and London: Routledge, 2015), pp. 168–231.
6. Laura A. Miller. *Reluctant Capitalists: Bookselling and the Culture of Consumption* (Chicago: University of Chicago Press, 2006), pp. 117–160. Also see Janice A. Radway. *A Feeling for Books: the Book-of-the-Month Club, Literary Taste, and Middle Class Desire* (Chapel Hill, NC: University of North Carolina Press, 1997), pp. 76–77, 84–85, 166–167. Jason Epstein. *Book Business: Publishing Past Present and Future* (New York: W.W. Norton, 2001), pp. 37–38, 161–169. Lewis A. Coser, Charles Kadushin, and Walter W. Powell. *Books: the Culture and Commerce of Publishing* (Chicago; University of Chicago Press, 1983), pp. 323–341. Dan Sinykin. *Big Fiction: How Conglomeration Changed the Publishing Industry and American Literature* (New York: Columbia University Press, 2023), pp. 24–25, 61–68.
7. Clayton M. Christensen. *The Innovator's Dilemma: The Revolutionary Book That Will Change the Way You Do Business* (New York: Harper Business, 2011), pp. xi–xxxii, 3–8, 33–58.
8. Albert N. Greco. *The Strategic Marketing of Science, Technology, and Medical Journals: A Business History of a Dynamic Marketplace, 2000–2020* (Cham, Switzerland, Palgrave Macmillan, 2023), pp. 24, 31–46.
9. Ibid. Also see Eugene Garfield. "The History and Meaning of the Journal Impact Factor," *Journal of the American Medical Association 295*, 1 (January 4, 2006); https://doi.org/10.1001/jama.295.1.90. Arthur G. Bedeian. "The Manuscript Review Process: The Proper Roles of Authors, Referees, and Editors," *Journal of Management Inquiry 12* (2003): 331–338. Mary Waltham. "The Future of Scholarly Journal

Publishing Among Social Science and Humanities Associations," *Journal of Scholarly Publishing 41*, 3(April 2010): 257–324. Cary Wu. "The Gender Citation Gap: Approaches, Explanations, and Implications," *Sociology Compass*; https://doi.org/10.1111/soc4.13189. Maureen Pirog. "Professional Practice: The Art and Science of Scholarly Publishing," *Journal of Policy Analysis and Management 33*, 3 (Summer2014): 843–853.

10. Computer History Museum. "Timeline of Computer History;" https://www.computerhistory.org/timeline/computers.

11. *The Guardian*. "The History of Smartphones: Timeline;" https://www.theguardian.com/technology/2012/jan/24/smartphones-timeline.

12. Zoom. "the Heart of Human Connection;" https://www.zoom.com/en/about.

13. The History Cooperative. "The Complete History of Social Media: A Timeline of the Invention of Online Networking;" https://historycooperative.org/the-history-of-social-media.

14. Patrick H. Alexander. "Thoughts About Open Access Publishing in a Humanities Context," *Journal of Eastern Mediterranean Archaeology and Heritage Studies 1*, 1(2013): 97–98. Also see John Houghton and Peter Sheehan. "Estimating the Potential Impacts of Open Access to Research Findings," *Economic Analysis and Policy 39*, 1(March 2009): 127–142.

15. Laura M. Stevens. "From The Editor: Getting What You Pay For? Open Access and the Future of Humanities Publishing," *Tulsa Studies in Women's Literature," 32*, 1(Spring 2013): 7–21. Also see Damien Besancenot and Radu Vranceanu. "A Model of Scholarly Publishing With Hybrid Academic Journals," *Theory and Decision 82*, 1(January 2017): 131–160.

16. Peter Suber. "A Very Brief Introduction to Open Access;" https://www.easrlham.edu/~peters/fos/overview.htm.

17. Ibid. Also see Seth S. Leopold. "Editorial: Paying to Publish—What Is Open Access and Why Is It Important?" https://doi.org/10.1007/s11999-014-3615-9. Also see John Willinsky. "The Access Principle: The Case for Open Access to Research and Scholarship;" https://repository.arizona.edu/handle/10150/106529.

18. *Suber*. Open Access (Cambridge, MA: MIT Press, 2012); https://doi.org/10.7551/mitpress/9286.001.0001. Also see Suber's 2005 article. "Promoting Open Access in the Humanities;" *Syllecta Classica*; https://doi.org/10.1353/syl.2005.000. Suber's 2004 article. "Creating an Intellectual Commons Through Open Access;" https://dlc.dlib.indiana.edu/dlc/bitstream/handle/10535/4445/Suber_Creating_041004.pdf.

19. David Solomon and Bo-Christer Bjork. "Article Processing Charges for Open Access Publications—The Situation for Research Intensive Universities in the U.S.A. and Canada;" https://doi.org/10.7717/peerrj.2264. Also see Angel Borrego. "Article Processing Charges for

Open Access Journal Publishing: A Review," *Learned Publishing 36*, 3(2023): 359–378.

20. *Academic Librarian.* "Notes on the Serials Crisis;" https://blogs.princeton.edy/librarian/2010/04/notes_on_the_serialscrisis. Also see Philip Young. "The Serials Crisis and Open Access: A White Paper for the Commission on Research, Virginia Tech," http://hdl.handle.net/10760/14118.

21. Jonathan G. Fairman. "The First and Second Laws of Motion," National Aeronautics and Space Administration (NASA); https://www.grc.nasa.gov/www/k-12/WindTunnel/Activities.first2nd_lawsf_motion.html.

22. Heather Morrison, Jihane Salhab, Alexis Calve-Genest, and Tony Horava. "Open Access Article Processing Charges: DOAJ Survey May 2014," Publications 2015 3: 1–16; https://doi.org/10.3390/publications.3010001.

23. Ibid.

24. Ibid.

25. Richard Van Noorden. "Open Access: The True Cost of Science Publishing," Nature 495 (2013): 426–429.

26. Ibid. Also see John Mackenzie Owen. "The New Dissemination of Knowledge: Digital Libraries and Institutional Roles in Scholarly Publishing," *Journal of Economic Methodology 9*, 3(November 2002): 275–288.

27. Peter Suber. "Open Access: Six Myths to Put to Rest," *The Guardian*; https://www.theguardian.com/higher-education-network/blog/2013/oct/21/open-access-myths-peter-suber-harvard.

28. Ibid.

29. Paul N. and Matthew Nielsen. "On The Cost of Keeping a Book;" https://textlibris.lib.utexas.edu/wp-content/uploads/2018/08/Courantand Nielsen.pdf.

30. *The Chronicle of Higher Education.* "Spending by University Research Libraries, 2012–2013;" https://www.chronicle.com/article/spending-by-university-research-libraries-2012-13/?sra=true. Also see Stephen E. Wiberley, Jr. "The Humanities: Who Won the 90s in Scholarly Book Publishing," *Portal: Libraries and the Academy, 2*, 3(2002): 357–374.

31. University of Florida. "University Libraries 2014–2015 Budget Year-to-Date, June 30, 2015;" https://businessservices.uflib.ufl.edu/wordpress/files/2020/04/06.15_UL.pdf.

32. Rutgers University. "Daily Record: Letter: Rutgers Should Restore Library Budget;" https://www.dailyrecord.com/story/opinion/letters/2014/11/02/rutgers-restore-library-budget/18258013.

33. American Library Association (ALA). "Library Operating Expenditures: A Selected Annotated Bibliography;" https://www.ala.org/tools/libfact-sheets/alalibraryfactsheet104. Also see American Library Association. "ALA releases 2014 State of America's Libraries Report;" https://www.prnewswire.com/news-releases/ala-releases-2014-state-of-americas-libraries-report-255108311.html.

34. Anne Ford. "When Universities Cut, Libraries Bleed: How Academic Libraries Respond to Shrinking Offerings;" https://americanlibrariesmag-azine.org/2018/11/01/when-universities-cut-libraries-bleed. Also see Association of Research Libraries (ARL), SPARC-ACRL Forum: Connecting Articles and Data to Expand Open Access to Research;" https://www.arl.org/event/sparc-acrl-forum-connecting-articles-and-data-to-expand-open-access-to-research.

CHAPTER 4

The Crisis in the Humanities and Scholarly Publishing: 2014–2024

Abstract Scholars have written about the "crisis in the humanities." However, in reality there were more than just one crisis. This book analyzed 11 distinct "crises in the humanities," including declines in college enrollments, increases in the number of college faculty members, the growth in the number of Ph.D. degrees awarded, declines in undergraduate student major in the humanities, declines in the number of master's students majoring in the humanities, declines in graduate school enrollments, financial concerns about college libraries, college financial issues, the impact of Covid on colleges, gender disparity, and declines in attendance and financial support for museums.

Keywords Crisis in the humanities • Two cultures • Student enrollment • College faculty • Humanities degrees • Humanities enrollment • Number of colleges • Covid • Gender disparity • Academic book output • Academic book prices • Humanities serials prices • U.S. Bookstores • Consumer Price Index

INTRODUCTION

The "crisis in the humanities" has been a dominant theme in the humanities literature. However, there was not one crisis that undermined the humanities academic fields. In reality, there were a "series of crises" that go back decades in the eclectic history of the humanities in the United States. And defining precisely the "crises" has been an intriguing endeavor. Fortunately, a number of prominent scholars provided the best intellectual overview of the "crises."

The first and perhaps the most important scholar to address the "crisis in the humanities" was C.P. Snow. In his famed May 1959 lecture, Snow outlined what he maintained was the development of two distinct cultures: the humanities and the sciences. "Literary intellectuals at one pole—at the other scientists, and as the most representative, the physical sciences. Between the two, a gulf of mutual incomprehension—sometimes particularly among the young, hostility and dislike."[1] Snow described these two poles in some detail. "At one pole, the scientific culture really is a culture, not only in an intellectual but also in an anthropological sense. That is, its members need not, and of course often do not, always completely understand each other."[2] "Remember, these are very intelligent men. Their culture is in many ways an exciting and admirable one. It doesn't contain much art, with the exception, an important exception, of music... Of books, though, very little."[3]

At the other pole, according to Snow in *The Two Cultures*, are the literary people. "A good many times, I have been present at gatherings of people who, by the standards of the traditional culture, are thought highly educated and who have with considerable gusto been expressing their incredulity at the illiteracy of scientists. Once or twice, I have been provoked and have asked the company how many of them could describe the Second law of Thermodynamics. The response was cold; it was also negative. Yet I was asking something which is about the scientific equivalent of: have you read a work of Shakespeare's?"[4]

When did the poles splinter into what could be called different if not hostile camps? Snow believed that "the two cultures were already dangerously separate sixty years ago [i.e., around 1899]... Thirty years ago [i.e., about 1929],the cultures had long ceased to speak to each other; but at least they managed a kind of frozen smile across the gulf. Now the politeness has gone; and they just make faces. It is not only that the young scientists now feel that they are part of a culture on the rise while the other is in retreat."[5]

Snow, in his widely circulated and influential lecture, viewed the literary intellectuals as "natural luddites."[6] Clearly, his view of a polarized academia sparked intense debates in England, Europe, and in the United States. "From the beginning, the phrase 'the two cultures' evoked some protests. The word 'culture' or 'cultures' has been objected to; so, with much more substance, has the number two..."[7] However, Snow insisted that "the phrase 'the two cultures' still seems appropriate for the purpose I had in mind."[8]

In conclusion, Snow was more optimistic. He stated that "I was talking primarily to educators and those being educated... Changes in education will not by themselves, solve our problems; but without these changes we shan't even realize what the problems are... The division of our culture is making us more obtuse than we need be... However, we can educate a large proportion of our better minds so that they are not ignorant of imaginative experience, both in the arts and in science."[9]

Other scholars commented positively on Snow's position. David Arndt's "The Two Cultures and the Crisis in the Humanities" outlined what he maintained were other causes that triggered a "crisis in the humanities," including "the humanities have become too specialized; work in the humanities has become too narrow, trivial, and insular; humanists write in a technical jargon that is opaque to outsiders; the humanities curriculum has become fragmented and incoherent; education in the humanities is adrift without any sense of common purpose; and the humanities have become increasingly irrelevant in a world dominated by modern science."[10]

In essence, Arndt believed that humanists, and the publishers of books and journals in the humanities, had to reevaluate the nature of the research that they wrote and published. "My basic argument is this: the modern sciences inspired the creation of the research university, and the research university is oriented by different aims and rests on different assumptions about the nature of truth, tradition, language, and education."[11] Arndt maintained that his essential "thesis, again, is that the humanities are thrown into crisis when they are detached from the liberal arts model of education, reinterpreted in light of the assumptions of the research model, cast in the mold of the modern sciences, and incorporated into the model of the research university... This hyper specialization [in the humanities] has led to narrow, insular, and trivial scholarship."[12]

The famed historian J.H. Plumb, in his 1964 book *Crisis in the Humanities*, also looked at recent historical developments to explain why there was a crisis in the humanities. He wrote that "the rising tide of scientific and industrial societies, combined with the battering of two World Wars, has shattered the confidence of humanities in their capacity to lead or instruct. Uncertain of their social function, their practitioners have taken refuge in two desperate courses—both suicidal. Either they blindly cling to their traditional attitudes and pretend that their function is what it was and that all will be well so long as change is repelled, or they retreat into their own private professional world and deny any social function to their subject. And so the humanities are at a crossroads, a crisis in their existence; they must either change the image they present, adopt themselves to the needs of society dominated by science technology, or retreat into social trivality."[13]

Plumb also addressed what he called the "historian's dilemma." "The rise of natural science deeply influenced historians. They admired the exactitude of science, the clarity of its arguments, even more than the certainty of its conclusions."[14] So what can historians do to address this crisis, this dilemma, in the humanities? Plumb wrote that "anyone with imagination and some scholarship can deepen his experience about the nature of man in society and the historical processes of change. He [i.e., either a male or a female historian] will not, of course in my own University of Cambridge be led directly to such considerations... He will be encouraged to read history."[15] The end result was rather depressing to Plumb; it was, after all, a continuation of the historian's intellectual isolation from the sciences and technology that led to a fragmentation, a crisis, in the humanities.

The intense, and at times, rather prickly, debate over the two cultures triggered a number of intriguing observations. Roger Kimball, writing in *The New Criterion*, addressed many of the issues raised by Snow. He believed that the debate over the two cultures "seems like a terrible muddle" since "Snow is especially impatient with the politics of the 'traditional culture'."[16] Kimball elaborated on his belief that "it is not simply that the gulf between scientists and literary intellectuals (and the general public, too, of course) has grown wider as science has become ever more specialized and complex... The gulf is unbridgeable and will only widen as knowledge progresses."[17]

Stanley Fish, writing in *The New York Times*, worried about the imbalance in the financing and elimination of pivotal humanities areas and departments in order to support the ever increasing demand of the sciences. "For someone of my vintage, the elimination of French [at SUNY Binghamton] was the shocker... French departments were the location of much of the intellectual energy. Faculty and students in other disciplines looked to French philosophers and critics for inspiration."[18] Fish asked what can be done to protect the humanities. And he was, basically, not optimistic about the future… "It won't do, in the age of entrepreneurial academics, zero-based budgeting, and 'every tub on its own bottom,' to ask computer science or biology or the medical school to fork over some of their funds so that the revenue-poor classics department can be maintained. That was the idea a while back, but today it won't fly."[19]

Marjorie Perloff remarked that "one of our most common genres today is the epitaph for the humanities… [But] the humanities are not one thing. They are all around us and evident in our daily lives."[20] Her solution was persuasive. "The arts and the humanities belong to all of the people of the United States… An advanced civilization must not limit its efforts to science and technology alone, but must give full value and support to the other great branches of scholarly and cultural activity in order to achieve a better understanding of the past, a better analysis of the present, and a better view of the future."[21]

The Crises: "Gradually, then Suddenly"[22]

While Snow, Plum, and the other scholars addressed the overarching problems that triggered a crisis in the humanities, fortunately, there is an abundance of data that highlights some of the substantive developments in the humanities after 2015.

First, the U.S. Department of Education (Education), National Center for Education Statistics (NCES) released college and graduate school enrollment tallies for 2014 to 2021 with projections for the years 2022–2028. Looking at the years 2014–2021, there was a -2.61% decrease in the total number of full-time students with a small +0.95% growth in the number of part-time students. So, total enrollment for 2014–2021 sagged -1.25%. Education and NCES were more optimistic about the years 2022–2028, probably relying on the standard Autoregressive Integrated Moving Average (ARIMA) forecasting model. However, one must be cautious when relying on forecasts, even from Education and NCES. A number of academics also addressed many of these concerns, including Leonard Cassuto, Paul Jay, and Julie R. Posselt.[23] Table 4.1 has the data for 2014–2021 as well as the projections for 2022–2028 and the overall projections for 2014–2028.

Second, the total number of full-time higher education faculty members between 2015 and 2022 tallied 6,826,955, up +15.61%. The number

Table 4.1 Total U.S. non-profit public and private college students 2014–2028

Year	Undergraduate and graduate students			Total annual percentage change
	Full-time	Part-time	Total	
2014	12,454,464	7,754,628	20,209,092	-0.82%
2015	12,287,512	7,700,692	19,988,204	-1.09%
2016	12,125,314	7,721,590	19,846,904	-0.71%
2017	12,077,304	7,688,294	19,765,598	-0.41%
2018	12,103,000	7,725,000	19,828,000	+0.32%
2019	12,135,000	7,768,000	19,904,000	+0.38%
2020	12,133,000	7,795,000	19,928,000	+0.12%
2021	12,129,000	7,828,000	19,956,000	+0.14%
2022	12,131,000	7,860,000	19,991,000	+0.18%
2023	12,145,000	7,895,000	20,040,000	+0.25%
2024	12,178,000	7,929,000	20,107,000	+0.33%
2025	12,220,000	7,557,000	20,177,000	+0.35%
2026	12,264,000	7,994,000	20,258,000	+0.40%
2027	12,272,000	8,023,000	20,295,000	+0.18%
2028	12,261,000	8,044,000	20,305,000	+0.05%
2014–2021 Percent change	-2.61%	+0.95%	-1.25%	–
2021–2028 Percent change	+1.07%	+2.34%	+1.57%	–
2014–2028 Percent change	-1.55%	+3.73%	+0.47%	–

U.S. Department of Education. National Center for Education Statistics, https://nces.ed.gov/programs/digest/d18/tables/dt18_303.10.asp

N.B. All numbers rounded off and may not always equal 100 percent. Data for 2022–2028 are estimates from the National Center for Education Statistics

of part-time faculty (i.e., non-tenure track faculty, sometimes called adjunct or contingent—they often are paid on a per-course salary and they rarely have access to medical-dental-vision care-retirements benefits available to full-time tenure track or tenured faculty)—topped with 5,792,424 and their percent change mirrored essentially the full-time growth rate with an increase of +15.63%. The ratio between full-time and part-time faculty varies during years; however, looking at the cumulative totals for 2015–2022, the percentage of full-time was 54.10% with the part-time total settling in at 45.92%.

The growth in the number of part-time faculty has been the subject of some controversy. While these part-timers often bring exceptional skill-sets and experiences to the classroom, clearly enriching the education of students, many full-time faculty, especially in the humanities, maintained that every teaching assignment offered to a part-timer was a course that could have, or should have, been offered to a full-time Ph.D. (especially to a new tenure track member) in possibly history, English language and literature, or philosophy since full-time positions in the humanities are often scarce. For example, James Monk, writing for the American Association of University Professors (AAUP) remarked that "part-time faculty are exploited, underpaid, and afforded miserable working terms and conditions is not a perception, it is a reality. They are paid less, work harder, have fewer benefits, have less protection, and are accorded less respect than full-time faculty."[24] Table 4.2 has the data.

Third, the growth in the number of individuals awarded the Ph.D. in all academic fields between 2015 and 2022 increased +10.56% (totaling 1,492,161; the average annual total was 186,520.13). Education and NCES data for doctoral degrees in all of the humanities was 120,533 (+2.97%). Annually, the humanities average for eight years was +8.08% (averaging 15,069.13 degrees). Table 4.3 has the totals.

Table 4.2   Number of higher education faculty: 2015–2022

Year	Full-time	Part-time	Total	Full-time percent	Part-time percent
2015	807,000	745,000	1,552,000	52.00%	48.00%
2016	814,000	732,000	1,546,000	52.65%	47.35%
2017	823,000	723,000	1,546,000	53.23%	46.77%
2018	832,000	711,000	1,543,000	53.92%	46.08%
2019	844,000	705,000	1,549,000	54.49%	45.51%
2020	937,000	653,000	1,590,000	58.93%	41.07%
2021	837,000	662,000	1,499,000	55.84%	44.16%
2022	932,955	861,424	1,794,379	51.99%	48.01%
2015–2022					
Total	6,826,955	5,792,424	12,619,379	–	–
Average	853,369.38	724,053.00	1,577,422.38	–	–
Annual percent change	+15.61%	+15.63%	+15.62%	54.10%	45.90%
Annual percent of total	51.99%	48.01%	100%	–	–

Source: *The Statistical Abstract of the United States*, various years
N.B. All numbers rounded off and may not always equal 100%

Looking at the always important academic field of English language and literature as a "typical" academic field in the humanities, Education and NCES reported that, between 2015 and 2018, the number of females (3355; 61.42%) earning the Ph.D. exceeded significantly the number of males (2107; 38.58%). However, all of the data in this field exhibited a -8.6% decline for those four years; and the number of females dropped a sharp -9.38%, and males experienced a -7.58% decline. Unfortunately, Education and NCES did not release data for females and males earning Ph.D. degrees for the years after 2018. Table 4.4 has the numbers.

As for the Ph.D. awarded in the other humanities disciplines, five academic areas were selected for analysis, based on data from Education and NCES, for the years 2014–2021. In the area, ethnic and cultural studies field, while 2600 degrees were granted, this academic area averaged 326.25 annually and sustained a rather dramatic -20.24% decline between 2014 and 2021. The growing communications and related programs

Table 4.3   Total number of doctoral degrees awarded in the United States and in the humanities: 2015–2022

Year	Total number of all doctoral degrees	Percent of humanities' doctoral degrees	Total number of doctoral degrees in the humanities
2015	178,548	8.7%	15,533
2016	177,867	8.6%	15,297
2017	181,357	8.1%	14,690
2018	183,734	7.9%	14,515
2019	187,577	7.8%	14,631
2020	190,178	7.7%	14,644
2021	195,500	7.8%	15,249
2022	197,400	8.1%	15,994
2015–2022			
Total	1,492,161	8.08%	120,533
Average	186,520.13	–	15,069.13
Percent change	+10.56%	–	+2.97%

Source: U.S. Department of Education. National Center for Education Statistics; https://nces.ed.gov/propgrams/digest/d17/tables/dt17_318.20.asp; https://nces.ed.gov/programs/digest/d12/tables/dt12_310.asp; The American Academy of Arts and Sciences. "Humanities' Share of All Advanced [Doctoral] Degrees Conferred"; https://www.amacad.org/humanities-indicators/higher-education/humanities-share-all-advanced-degrees-conferred; *The Statistical Abstract of the United States*; various years
N.B. Excludes professional degrees. All numbers rounded off and may not always equal 100%. Projections for 2019–2022

Table 4.4 Number of males and females earning the Ph.D. degree in English language and literature: 2015–2018

Year	Totals	Total number of males	Total number of females	Percent of total	
				Males	Females
2015	1418	554	864	39.07%	60.93%
2016	1402	522	880	37.23%	62.77%
2017	1347	519	828	38.53%	61.47%
2018	1295	512	783	39.54%	60.46%
2015–2018 Total	5462	2107	3355	–	–
2015–2018 Percent change	-8.67%	-7.58%	-9.38%	–	–
2015–2018 Percent of total	–	–	–	38.58%	61.42%

Source: U.S. Department of Education (education). National center for Education Statistics (NCES): https://nces.ed.gov/programs/digest/d19/tables/dt19_325.50.asp?current=yes

N.B. Data not available from NCES for the years after 2018

(including journalism and publishing) had 4882 degrees (610.25 annually), but it also experienced a smaller -12.93% drop between 2014 and 2021. Data for English language and literature was available through 2021. While this is a large academic field (10,493 degrees; 1311.65 annually), there was a staggering decline in degrees of -22.54% for 2014–2021. Foreign language and literature also suffered through an unfortunate decline of -19.98% with 9478 degrees (1184.75 annually). Rounding out these five categories was philosophy and religion studies, accounting for 5748 Ph.D. degrees (-10.17%) while averaging 718.50. Table 4.5 has the data.

Fourth, four important and typical undergraduate majors were investigated for the years 2014 and 2021. English language and literature, generally the largest major in the humanities, recorded 283,119 bachelor's degrees (averaging annually 40,445.57). As with the doctoral data, English suffered through a steep -22.00% decline in the number of degrees awarded. While foreign language and literature is a popular major, with 120,961 degrees (with an annual average of 17,280.14), it also experienced a -20.39% decline during those seven years. The combined philosophy and religious studies field exhibited some very positive results: 76,407

Table 4.5 A selected number of doctoral degrees awarded in the humanities: 2014–2021

Year	Total number of humanities' doctorates in academic fields and sub-fields				
	Area ethnic, cultural & studies	Communications & related programs	English language & literature	Foreign language & literature	Philosophy & religious studies
2014	336	611	1393	1231	698
2015	312	644	1418	1243	762
2016	316	629	1402	1265	746
2017	349	615	1347	1168	741
2018	335	666	1295	1213	768
2019	370	583	1274	1211	712
2020	324	602	1285	1162	694
2021	268	532	1079	985	627
2014–2021					
Total	2,610.00	4882	10,493	9478	5748
Average	326.25	610.25	1311.65	1184.75	718.50
Percent change	-20.24%	-12.93%	-22.54%	-19.98%	-10.17%

Source: U.S. Department of Education, National Center for Education Statistics; https://nces.gov.edu/programs/digect/d17/tables/d17_318.20.asp.;   https://nces.ed.gov/programs/digest/d21/tables/d21_318.20.asp.; *The Statistical Abstract of the United States*; various years

N.B. The year "2014" refers to the academic year 2013–2014. "Communications & journalism & related programs" also refers to publishing studies. "History and the Social Sciences" were consolidated and were excluded. All numbers rounded off and may not always equal 100%

degrees (averaging 10,915.28); this was the only field with a positive growth rate (+8.28%) between 2015 and 2021. Unfortunately, theology and religious vocations dropped an unnerving -30.64% on 59,209 degrees (averaging annually only 8458.43). It is possible that this decline was because of a reduction in the number of religious vocations and/or concerns about the costs of degrees. Table 4.6 has the details.

Fifth, data about master's degrees posted results remarkably similar to the same four categories as the bachelor's data. English language and literature, with 57,978 degrees (averaging 8282.57 annually) slipped -12.07%. Foreign language and literature also declined -19.69% (with a total of 22,378) averaging annually 3196.86. Philosophy and religious studies was the only bright spot, +8.42% awarding 13,797 degrees (averaging 1971.00). Theology and religious vocations posted better results

Table 4.6   A selected number of humanities bachelor's degrees: 2015–2021

Year	English language and literature	Foreign language and literature and linguistics	Philosophy and religious studies	Theology and religious vocations
2015	45,851	19,493	11,071	9713
2016	42,797	18,436	10,155	9804
2017	41,314	17,643	9,711	9518
2018	40,002	16,957	9,603	9521
2019	39,344	16,605	11,981	7061
2020	38,049	16,309	11,898	6855
2021	35,762	15,518	11,988	6737
2015–2021				
Total	283,119	120,961	76,407	59,209
Average	40,445.57	17,280.14	10,915.29	8458.43
Percent change	-22.00%	-20.39%	+8.28%	-30.64%

Source: *The Statistical Abstract of the United States*, various years
N.B. History data was combined with the social sciences. All numbers rounded off

than their undergraduate counterpart off only -7.31% on impressive 94,861 number of degrees (13,551.57 annual average). Table 4.7 has the details.

Sixth, gradual then sudden declines in undergraduate and graduate school enrollments, when coupled with increase in the number of higher education faculty members and the number of doctoral degrees in the humanities, created a potential financial problem for many colleges and universities. Financial concerns, along with a few others, exacerbated the "crises in the humanities."

Between 2011 and 2021, statistical data from Education and NCES revealed a decline in the number of public and private (non-profit) higher education institutions in the United States. In 2011, there were 2015 public and 1812 private (3827) colleges and universities in this nation. By 2021, those totals were lower: public declined -6.10%, bottoming out at 1892; private institutions sagged -3.20% to 1754. Other research studies also addressed these declines, including the Hechinger Report.[25] Table 4.8 has the annual data.

In addition, a number of higher education institutions started to reduce (called "right-sizing" in many university press releases) certain programs in the humanities because of declines in enrollments. These developments

Table 4.7   A selected number of humanities master's degrees: 2015–2021

Year	English language and literature	Foreign language and literature and linguistics	Philosophy and religious studies	Theology and religious vocations
2015	8928	3566	1912	14,271
2016	8577	3405	1756	14,352
2017	8244	3271	1704	13,694
2018	8300	3261	1893	13,828
2019	8217	3081	2280	12,842
2020	7862	2930	2179	12,646
2021	7850	2864	2073	13,228
2015–2021				
Total	57,978	22,378	13,797	94,861
Average	8282.57	3196.86	1971.00	13,551.57
Percent change	-12.07%	-19.69%	+8.42%	-7.31%

Source: *The Statistical Abstract of the United States*, various years

N.B. Data for history was combined with the social sciences. All numbers rounded off

Table 4.8   Number of higher education institutions in the United States: 2011–2021

Year	Number of public institutions	Number of private institutions (non-profit)	Totals	Annual percentage change
2011	2015	1812	3827	–
2012	2011	1830	3841	+0.37%
2013	1981	1820	3801	-1.04%
2014	1980	1834	3814	+0.34%
2015	1964	1827	3791	-0.60%
2016	1965	1859	3624	+0.87%
2017	1958	1823	3781	-1.12%
2018	1955	1826	3781	–
2019	1952	1780	3732	-1.30%
2020	1933	1774	3707	-0.67%
2021	1892	1754	3646	-1.65%
2011–2021 Percent change	-6.10%	-3.20%	-4.73%	–

Source: U.S. Department of Education. National Center for Education Statistics

and trends were addressed in a series of major studies. Christopher John Newfield, the president of the influential Modern Language Association (MLA), wrote on August 10, 2022, that the "crisis in the humanities" should be viewed "as a funding crisis" that impacted negatively research endeavors in the humanities. "An essential piece of research infrastructure is facing cuts.... The National Endowments for the Humanities (NEH) had an overall budget of $180 million... a bit more than ten percent of the budget went to research... And yet the very small share allocated to basic research signals that sponsoring research is not the main activity of the federal government's only agency dedicated to the humanities."[26]

The College Art Association (CAA) listed a series of colleges that "have taken steps to reduce or cut arts and humanities programs, faculty positions, or institutions on campus, including the University of Wisconsin—Stevens Point, California State University—Chico, the University of Southern Maine, and SUNY—Stony Brook.[27] Nick Anderson, writing in *The Washington Post*, described the unanimous decision of Marymount University's Board of Trustees to "phase out majors in English, history, and several other fields that the Catholic school in Northern Virginia have drawn low student interest... [This decision] represents a watershed moment for a regional university of almost 3,700 students... It also shows the continuing vulnerability of humanities in higher education at a time when pressure is high to deliver degrees that many students and families perceive as more valuable in the job market."[28] However, small regional universities were not the only ones under financial pressure. "West Virginia University's student population has been shrinking for years... Now facing a $45 million budget deficit, administrators have proposed eliminating dozens of programs, including the mathematics Ph.D. degree and the entire world languages department."[29]

Seventh, academic programs were not the only areas subject to financial review and possible elimination. The academic library was also evaluated for possible reductions in financial support. Libraries faced herculean fiscal challenges, including increasing costs for wages and benefits and the funds needed to maintain a library (e.g., utilities, insurance, cleaning services, repairs, etc.).

The University of Arizona Library released detailed data about their operations. Their library allocations were as follows: "campus allocations" (i.e., direct financial support from the university: 62%); student fees: 30%; various gifts and grants: 6%; and the "other" category: 2%. Expenses were allocated as follows: staffing and related benefits: 40%; operations and other expenses (e.g., cleaning, utilities, etc.): 21%;, and "information access:" 39%. The library's total budget in 2023 was $30 million. As a comparison, Arizona's report also revealed that the Penn State University library budget was $60 million.[30]

While these university library budgets were impressive, the impact of changes in student enrollment and increased costs triggered many university to either not increase library budgets (which in a period of inflation was a de facto cut) or to reduce the library budget. Anne Ford wrote that "when a university cuts majors, programs, or even an entire school, what happens to the library? The obvious answer: nothing good. As universities across the country trim offerings... academic libraries must attempt to maintain services."[31] Ford interviewed academic librarians at a number of institutions (e.g. the University of Wisconsin—Superior; the University of Southern Maine; and Rider University, in New Jersey). All of the librarians indicated that programs were cut to address fiscal shortfalls.[32] Rutgers University announced it planned to cut the library budget by $550,000.00. The Rutgers *Daily Record* posted information about the cut. "When considering the annual inflation of [scholarly journal] subscription fees, this budget cut amounts to an $800,000.00 cut in the collections budgets alone. Additionally, the [Rutgers] libraries have to shoulder an annual $300,000.00 fee for becoming a member of the Big Ten's academic consortium, with no assistance from the university's unrestricted reserves."[33]

Clearly, cuts to library budgets impacted students, faculty, staff, and allocations for and use of books and journals in the library or through remote online library access. Amy Res, writing in *Library Journal* (*LJ*), analyzed a survey of 1843 college and university libraries. "Making collections of one [academic] library available to users of another has expanded from its origins in interlibrary loans (ILL) to sharing technical capabilities, staff skills and knowledge, discovery tools, collection management, and other resources."[34] In another *LJ* report analyzing "College Student Library Usage Survey Report 2022," *LJ* asked students "in the last year, have you used your school's library or library resources to support classwork in any of the following subjects?" The results about the humanities were revealing: 21.4% of the respondents used the English literature collection. The other percentages were rather low: history: 12.7%, the arts: 12.4%, communications: 9.7%, philosophy, religion, and theology: 6.0%, ethnic or gender studies: 5.2%, and languages other than English: 4.7%.[35]

Many of the findings in the *LJ* reports and surveys were confirmed in a series of major studies, including important reports released by the

Association of College Research Libraries (ACRL): "Top Trends in Academic Libraries," "2020 ACRL Academic Library Trends and Statistics Survey," "2020 Top Trends in Academic Libraries," and "Top Issues Facing Academic Libraries: A Report of the Focus on Future Task Force."[36]

Danielle Cooper, Catherine Bond Hill, and Roger C. Schoenfeld in "Aligning the Research Library to Organizational Strategy" also addressed substantive trends impacting academic libraries. Based on their research, the authors evaluated the impact on universities and by extension academic libraries to support the increased emphasis on STEM (i.e., science, technology, engineering, and technology), computation, big data, and machine learning. So, what should university libraries expect in this changing research environment? The authors insisted that "ultimately, university leaders expressed widely varying expectations of the library... A final characteristic sought by [some] university leaders was for the library director to take responsibility for resource stewardship."[37] In essence, library directors, facing cuts to the library budget, should develop creative fiscal policies, and in many instances that meant doing more with less. And the library directors at many higher education institutions were compelled to initiate a review of the cost of books and scholarly journals.

Eighth, many higher educational institutions and academic librarians had to start evaluating their mission in light of increased financial pressures. This sparked an interest in utilizing traditional accounting and financial metrics in viewing their collection and the increasing costs to purchase and maintain their book and journal collections. In essence, librarians had to start thinking about issues normally studied and analyzed in business schools (and not in library science degree programs), specifically the nature of supply and demand.[38] What books and scholarly journals did students and faculty need? And could a library allocate enough funds to match the demand for information (from faculty and students) against the supply of funds available to cover these expenses?

Looking at four important book categories in the humanities for the years 2014–2021, librarians observed additional increases in new title output and especially in the suggested retail price (SRP) for these books. In the fine and applied arts category, new title output reached 61,668 during those eight years, averaging annually 7708 (+8.27%). The average annual SRP was $73.89 (+22.28% between 2014 and 2021). The second book category was history; new title output topped 115,621, averaging annually 14,452.63 (+22.04% during those years). The SRP for history was $74.87 (+12.99% by 2021). The new books in the consolidated language and literature category were a staggering 214,291 (averaging 30,613.04; +12.06%). The SRP was $58.25, an increase of +15.08% over the years in the table. The last category was philosophy and religion: 92,480 new titles, averaging 11,560.00, and the SRP was $82.63 (+9.1%). Table 4.9 has all of the details. While new title output and prices increased, librarians, utilizing computer systems to track how often a book circulated, discovered there was a decline in faculty and student use of and demand for books. Table 4.9 has the details.

Looking at five categories in the scholarly journal sector, the SRP for a subscription for arts and architecture journals was $442.32, +97.17% between 2014 and 2022. History's SRP was lower at $404.04 (+70.59%). Other smaller SRPs were posted by language and literature ($397.43; +66.11%); music ($282.75; +50.92%); and philosophy and religion ($385.81; +51.99%). Clearly, the demand from faculty members and students for access to scholarly journals placed many librarians in a bind since the cost of serials increased every time a new contract was negotiated with a publisher. Table 4.10 has the data.

Libraries purchase new and used books from a variety of sources, including directly buying titles from the publisher, online websites (especially for deeply discounted used books), and sometimes from local or national bookstores (i.e., Barnes & Noble). The total number of bookstores in the United States declined -31.58% between 2015 and 2020; data was not available for the years after 2020. However, total revenues were available for bookstores from the U.S. Department of Commerce (Commerce), Bureau of the Census (Census); and the data indicated revenues declined -21.71% during those years. Table 4.11 has the tallies. The Federal Reserve

Bank of Minneapolis released annual changes in the Consumer Price Index (CPI) for "All Urban Consumers" between 2014 and 2023. The CPI increased +28.73% and this change impacted libraries trying to balance income versus expenditures. Table 4.12 has the CPI data for these ten years. Librarians also investigated the revenues of a number of publishers of scholarly books and journals. Looking at the years 2015 and 2022, the CPI was +23.50% during those years. Book and journal and some "other" revenue streams for two publishing companies were higher than the CPI: Informa (+25.23%), and both Springer and Cambridge University Press exhibited an increase (+30.00%). Elsevier's (RELXs) total was close to the CPI increase (+21.50%). John Wiley's increase was +14.29%. Two companies posted declines in total revenues: Wolters Kluwer (-10.46%) and Oxford University Press (-2.63%). Table 4.13 has the data.

Table 4.9 Academic book title output (units) and average prices in the humanities: 2014–2021 (U.S. dollars)

Year	Fine & applied arts		History		Language & literature		Philosophy & religion	
	Titles	Prices	Titles	Prices	Titles	Prices	Titles	Prices
2014	7561	$66.92	12,375	$70.61	27,054	$57.7	9390	$80.69
2015	8592	$67.71	15,412	$70.43	32,304	$55.87	12,035	$81.53
2016	8201	$67.85	15,419	$66.25	38,506	$44.49	10,698	$79.68
2017	8119	$72.22	14,380	$74.42	28,485	$62.65	11,985	$81.17
2018	5859	$77.19	13,470	$78.64	27,174	$62.36	11,369	$83.89
2019	7694	$74.66	15,105	$73.36	30,452	$58.25	12,153	$80.10
2020	7456	$82.74	14,357	$85.45	30,316	$66.40	12,020	$85.98
2021	8186	$81.83	15,103	$79.78	N/A	N/A	12,830	$88.07
	2014–2021		2014–2021		2014–2020		2014–2021	
Total	61,668	$591.12	115,621	$598.94	214,291	$407.72	92,480	$661.01
Annual average	7708.50	$73.89	14,452.63	$74.87	30,613.04	$58.25	11,560.00	$82.63
Percent change	+8.27%	+22.28%	+22.04%	+12.99%	+12.06%	+15.08%	+36.63%	+9.15%

Source: American Library Association

N.B. These are average prices; these totals do not include any discounts offered by publishers and/or distributors. All numbers rounded off. The language and literature data for 2021 in this table was listed by the ALA in its 2021 report. However, the totals seem "unusual," and might be revised in the ALA 2022 data. Therefore the tallies for this book category were only for 2014–2020

Table 4.10   Average price of humanities serials: 2014–2022 (U.S. dollars)

Year	Arts & architecture	History	Language & literature	Music	Philosophy & religion
2014	$290.00	$308.00	$303.00	$231.00	$307.00
2015	$297.00	$297.00	$310.00	$223.00	$309.00
2016	$299.52	$308.47	$318.02	$229.78	$338.79
2017	$322.75	$322.44	$337.01	$243.38	$360.10
2018	$462.80	$426.69	$416.04	$294.67	$394.85
2019	$487.41	$457.60	$440.67	$309.06	$414.81
2020	$523.95	$484.11	$465.55	$327.06	$432.90
2021	$545.64	$506.67	$483.22	$338.20	$448.19
2022	$571.78	$525.42	$503.32	$348.63	$466.62
2014–2022					
Total	$3800.85	$3636.40	$3576.83	$2544.78	$3472.26
Average	$442.32	$404.04	$397.43	$282.75	$385.81
Percent change	+97.17%	+70.59%	+66.11%	+50.92%	+51.99%

Source: American Library Association
N.B. These are average prices; these totals do not includes any discounts offered by publishers and/or distributors. All numbers rounded off

Table 4.11   U.S. bookstores: 2015–2022 and bookstore annual revenues: 2015–2022 ($ billions)

Year	Total number of bookstores	Annual bookstore revenues
2015	15,785	$10.88
2016	12,297	$10.59
2017	11,432	$10.33
2018	10,948	$9.54
2019	10,055	$8.96
2020	10,800	$6.19
2021	N/A	$8.02
2022	N/A	$8.35
2023	N/A	$8.30
	2015–2020	**2015–2023**
Total	71,317	$81.16
Annual average	11,886.17	$9.02
Percent change	-31.58%	-21.71%

Source: *The Bowker Annual* and the *Library and Book Trade Almanac*; various years. U.S. Department of Commerce, Bureau of the Census. https://www.census.gov/retail/index.html. U.S. Department of Commerce, Bureau of the Census. https://www.census.gov/retail/index.html
N.B.: The total number of bookstores includes the total number of chain and independent bookstores selling new and used books. All numbers rounded off and may not always equal 100%. In the United States, "bookstores" include a wide variety of retail establishments, including antiquarian, chains, college, independents, religious, used, etc. Bookstore totals were not available for all years. N/A for 2021–2023

One strategy that was employed by a growing number of academic libraries was to bring supply and demand into some type of equilibrium. Alia Wong, writing in *The Atlantic*, stated that "schools have been on a mission to reinvent campuses libraries… Some colleges see libraries as prime real estate that can hold any number of miscellaneous student services, from tutoring to day care."[39] Dan Cohen, also in *The Atlantic*, remarked that "university libraries around the world are seeing precipitous declines in the use of the books on their shelves… Yale recently decided to relocate three-quarters of the books in its undergraduate library to create more study space."[40] Cohen wrote that Yale and many other academic libraries experienced the same situation. For example, "college students at UVA [the University of Virginia] checked out 238,000 books during the school academic year a decade ago [i.e., this article was written in 2020; Cohen was referring to 2010]. Last year [i.e., in 2019] that number had shrunk to just 60,000."[41] This represented a stark decline of -74.79% at this library. The end result, to Cohen, was the decline of printed book use by students because of the emergence, availability, and wide acceptance by students of digital e-books.

Cohen's thesis was supported by a major research study from the Association of College and Research Libraries (ACRL), specifically the "2021 ACRL Academic Library Trends and Statistics Survey." The survey reported on the results of data from 1533 academic libraries covering the years 2019–2021. The key findings were significant. The average allocations for library salaries and fringe benefits were as follows: 2019: $1,711,588; 2020: $1,700,233; and for 2021: $1,592,965. This trend revealed a -6.93% reduction in salaries. Materials and services (which included the purchase of books and journal subscription fees) were 2019: $1,586,424; 2020: $1,551,442; and 2021: $1,554,980. The decline was -1.98%. The costs for operations and maintenance were: 2019: $435,986; 2020: $393,804; and 2021: $341,675; and this represented a decline of -21.6%.[42] The CPI for those years was +5.98%. Clearly, these 1533 academic libraries sustained a decline in their ability to keep pace with the ravages of inflation.

A possible answer to some of the problems plaguing academic libraries was in a major research study by Paul N. Courant and Matthew Nielsen at the University of Texas. These two authors analyzed what was clearly a foggy maze of 2009 library statistics and they asked the pithy question:[43] how much does it cost a library to keep one copy of a printed book on the

Table 4.12   Consumer price index 2014–2023

Year	Annual average CPI:	Annual percent change
	All urban consumers	Rate of inflation
2014	236.7	1.6%
2015	237.0	0.1%
2016	240.0	1.3%
2017	245.1	2.1%
2018	251.1	2.4%
2019	255.7	1.8%
2020	258.8	1.2%
2021	271.0	4.7%
2022	292.7	8.0%
2023	304.7	4.1%
2014–2023 Percent change	+28.73%	–

Source: Federal Reserve Bank Minneapolis; https://www.minneapolisfed.org/abouit-us/monetary-policy/inflation-calculator/consumer-price-index-1913

Table 4.13   Annual revenues for major commercial publishers and university presses (U.S. dollars in millions)

Year	RELX	Wolters Kluwer	John Wiley	Springer	Informa	Oxford University Press	Cambridge University Press
2015	$5.21	$4.59	$1.82	$1.61	$1.07	$1.14	$0.40
2016	$4.86	$3.38	$1.73	$1.72	$0.96	$0.94	$0.33
2017	$5.61	$3.99	$1.72	$1.96	$1.23	$1.14	$0.41
2018	$5.28	$3.76	$1.80	$1.99	$1.67	$1.07	$0.40
2019	$5.64	$3.98	$1.80	$1.93	$1.12	$1.11	$0.43
2020	$5.89	$4.33	$1.83	$2.00	$1.17	$1.03	$0.56
2021	$5.72	$4.62	$1.94	$1.92	$1.21	$1.05	$0.52
2022	$6.33	$4.11	$2.08	$2.06	$1.34	$1.11	N/A
2015–2022 Annual percent change	+21.50%	-10.46%	+14.29%	+27.95%	+25.23%	-2.63%	+30.00%

Source: *Publishers Weekly*, various issues. N.B.: 2023 totals not available
These totals include revenues from books, scholarly journals, APCs, reprints, etc

library's shelves? Their conclusion was dramatic: in 2009 it cost $3.15 for each book.[44] Looking at changes in the CPI, the $3.15 reached $4.58 in 2023.

Out of necessity, many libraries started to utilize the Courant-Nielsen research in order to evaluate their per-book shelf costs. Using the University of Illinois as an example, this library system in 2023 maintained a collection of more than 14,000,000 printed books.[45] Using the annual increase in the CPI as a metric (i.e., an annual cost of $4.58 for each book shelved in the library), Illinois' library spent $64.12 million in 2023 just to keep these books on the shelves.

It may seem incredulous that academic libraries would employ what librarians call "weeding" (i.e., the "deaccession") based on the age of a book, its circulation, and the need to allocate more space in the library for "other" activities or purposes. Laura Rice and Caroline Covington, writing in the *Texas Standard*, remarked that academic libraries "had to adapt dramatically to stay relevant and useful for students and their other patrons… Budgets have not changed much, but services have …If materials are going online, there is just new spaces and new opportunities."[46] Michael Rubinkam, in *The Christian Science Monitor*, wrote that "libraries are putting books in storage, contracting with resellers, or simply recycling them… Though 'weeding' has always taken place at libraries, experts say the pace is picking up. Finances are one factor…the digitization of books and other printed materials [i.e., scholarly journals] has dramatically affected the way students [and faculty members] do research."[47] Mary E. Miller and Suzanne M. Ward, in *The American Libraries Magazine*, also pointed out that library "collections were built on a just-in-case basis over the course of centuries… This was the best strategy to ensure access."[48] Matthew J. Jabaily, James R. Rodgers, and Steven A. Knowlton remarked that new sophisticated analytical processes can aid libraries in the "weeding' process. "Traditionally, usage figures for electronic serials have lumped all years of publication together. New tools give librarians information about usage according to the year of publication. They allow us to analyze the usage of current material separately from usage of content published in prior years… [This] may be helpful in reevaluating such subscription decisions."[49]

Ninth, starting in early 2020, the United States, and indeed the world, suffered through an outbreak of Covid-19, a debilitating and dangerous virus that killed millions of people in North America and the rest of the world. Higher education institutions, libraries, museums, archives, and the majority of retail establishments closed. The majority of U.S. colleges were able to go remote, using "Zoom" type systems to continue classroom instruction. The movement toward remote instruction was addressed in a series of important scholarly articles. Brennan Klein, Nicholas Generous, Matteo Chinazzi, Zaranna Bhadricha, Rishab Gunashekar, Preeti Kori, Bodian Li, Stefan McCabe, Jon Geen, David Lazer, Christopher R. Marsicano, Samuel V. Scarpino, and Alessandro Vespignani analyzed higher education response to the Covid menace in a major PLOS article. The Covid pandemic "has upended personal, public, and institutional life and has forced many to make decisions with limited data on how to best protect themselves and their communities."[50]

The impact of Covid and the movement toward remote learning on college students was analyzed by Alan R. Hamlin and Steve T. Barney. These two authors wrote that "universities have altered curriculum, changed [education] delivery methods, provided counseling, purchased new technology, and altered attendance policy."[51] The National Student Clearinghouse Research Center reported that many colleges and universities sustained both short-term and long-tern enrollment and financial declines.[52] Phillip W. Magness reported that students were forced to leave their dorm rooms, taking whatever clothing and personal property they could carry out the front door, leaving, unfortunately, their friends, social life, books, and research notes.[53]

This separation from traditional college classes and life, starting sometime in March 2020, lasted for some time (perhaps until the Fall 2021 semester). And this pandemic's impact lasted for years according to a major research study by Kesong Hu, Kaylene Godfrey, Qiping Ren, Shenlian Wang, Xuemei Yang, and Qi Li.[54]

MORE SEVERE AND LONG-TERM CRISES: THE IMPACT OF GENDER DISPARITY IN THE HUMANITIES

Tenth, the Covid situation was unfortunately just another substantive crisis that impacted female academics in the humanities, which included pay, promotion, publishing, hiring, service requirements, and teaching. Senait Fisseha, Gita Sen, Tedros Adhanom Ghebreyesus, Winnie Byanyima, Debora Diniz, Henrieta H. Fore, Natalia Kanem, Ulrika Karlsson, Rajat, Khosla, Laura Laski, Dina Mired, Phumzile Mlambo-Ngcuka, Tlanemg Mofokeng, Geeta Rao Gupta, Achim Steiner, Michelle Remme, and

Pascale Allotney, in *The Lancet*, remarked that the Covid-19 pandemic's "direct impacts have been compounded by pervasive gender inequalities with profound consequences especially for women... To control Covid-19 and mitigate its impacts, we need to tackle the structural determinants of gender inequality... This approach will be essential if we are to have a fighting chance to prevent the erosion and reversal of hard-won health and gender equality gains."[55] David Fang, Sonia K. Kang, and Sarah Kaplan, also in *The Lancet*, addressed the impact of Covid on gender inequality. They believed "the potential negative gendered consequences remain under-acknowledged. When women work from home, they report a disproportionate increase in domestic labor, childcare-related disruptions, and declines in productivity."[56]

A pivotal concern centers on whether female academics published fewer journal articles or books during the pandemic. Giuliana Viglione, in *Nature*, wrote that

> early analyses suggest that female academics are posting fewer preprints and starting fewer research projects than their male peers... Quarantined with a six-year old child underfoot, Megan Frederickson wondered how academic [females] were managing to write papers during the Covid-19 pandemic... Many households worldwide had become an intersection of work, school, and home life... The results are consistent with the literature on the division of childcare between men and women... Even in those dual-academic households, the evidence shows that women perform more household labor than men do.[57]

Anna Fazackerley, in *The Guardian*, reported that "in April [2020] Dr. Elizabeth Hannon, deputy editor of the *British Journal for the Philosophy of Science*, noticed that the number of article submissions she was receiving from women had dropped dramatically. Not so from men." She posted this observation on Twitter. "The response was an outpouring of recognition from frustrated female academics, saying they were barely coping with childcare and work during the coronavirus lockdown.... [Hannon writes that] having articles published in academic journals is key to being promoted at many universities."[58]

Other studies analyzed gender disparity in the humanities and related areas. Kim Eckart investigated if there were a glass ceiling in academic publishing that was limiting the number of females serving as editors or on editorial boards.[59] The impact of salary discrimination or female academics has long been a subject of debate and analysis. Donna K. Ginther and Kathy J. Haves addressed this issue in a landmark study published in the

American Economic Review in 1959.[60] A 2020 study released by the National Humanities Center stated that

> women faculty remain underrepresented at top tier research universities... and are paid approximately 20% less than their male colleagues. Compounding these issues, women faculty also engage in a disproportionate amount of service work, reducing available time for research activities and publishing. And, while the scholarly production of academic men does not decrease at all once they become fathers, academic women witness a sharp decline in their [scholarly] productivity as a result of the unequal demands placed on women caring for young children.[61]

The publication gender gap was investigated by Cary Wu. Wu wrote that "women tend to accumulate fewer citations over time and at the career level... [Wu] suggests that the primary reason for the lower citation rates at the author level is women publishing fewer articles over their careers... [Wu addressed] the potential detrimental impact of lower citations on women's career progression and the ways to address the issue to mitigate gender inequalities."[62]

Amanda Heidt, in *Nature*, wrote that "discrimination against members of under-represented groups in academic publishing leads to lower citation rates, fewer editorial-board positions, and longer manuscript review periods."[63] Alexander Michael Petersen, Santo Fortunato, Raj K. Pan, Kimmon Kaski, Orion Penner, Armando Rungi, Massimo Riccaboni, H. Eugene Stanley, and Fabio Pammolli wrote that scholarly publications, citations, and reputation are the key to a successful academic career; and publications impact a scholar's reputation in the field.[64] In many ways, an academic's career path is complicated since it can be based on the academic's "pedigree" which can impact the hiring process, and the type of institution that hires individuals with Ph.D. degrees from certain universities. John M. Herbert wrote that "astonishingly, if not entirely surprising, twenty percent of universities in the U.S. produce eighty percent of all domestically trained faculty, with just five institutions responsible for educating one in eight tenure-track faculty members at doctoral institutions."[65] K. Hunter Wapman, Sam Zhang, Aaron Clauset, and Daniel B. Larremore also addressed the hiring situation in "Quantifying Hierarchy and Dynamics in U.S. Faculty Hiring and Retention." These researchers examined "tenured or tenure-track faculty employed in the years 2011–2022 at 368 Ph.D. granting universities in the United States... [Their research findings indicated that] gains in women's representation over this decade [i.e., since 2020] result from demographic turnover and earlier changes made to hiring, and are unlikely to lead to long-term gender parity in most [academic] fields."[66]

The scholarly literature revealed yet another form of gender bias: faculty teaching evaluations. Ryan Quinn, writing in 2023 in *Inside Higher Education*, reported that "a study published this month adds to the many concerns about judging faculty members using student evaluations of their teaching. But this one suggests that gender imbalances in departments exacerbate the issue."[67] Colleen Flaherty, also in that same publication but in 2022, addressed different studies; and she wrote that "two new studies on gender bias in student evaluations of teaching look at the phenomenon from fresh—and troubling—angles… Finding that older female instructors were rated lower than younger women."[68]

The 11th crisis that impacted the humanities centered on the plight of humanities oriented museums, which are community anchors serving the public. Often working closely with local schools and universities, museums closed during the pandemic. The American Alliance of Museums (AAM) reported that "the pandemic has inflicted profound damage on U.S. museums, the vast majority of which are 501(c)(3) nonprofit charitable organizations…. Survey data shows two-thirds of museums continue [as of 2023] to experience reduced attendance; these institutions average 71% of their pre-pandemic attendance. Financial recovery from the damage of the pandemic has been inconsistent, with 30% of museums seeing decreased operating performance."[69]

The Metropolitan Museum of Art in New York City, one of the nation's preeminent museums, reported declines in attendance and endowment support while facing increased demands for the museum's total operating budget.[70] Clearly, if this world-renowned museum has financial difficulties, the vast majority of small, local museums face the specter of significant reductions in operating hours and staffing.

Conclusion

The "crisis in the humanities" is, in reality, at least 11 major crises that undermined the current, and future, state of the humanities in the United States. While some of these crises are beyond the ability of humanities departments, programs, and faculty members, specifically national changes in college enrollments, a number of the crises can be addressed by faculty and administrators. For example, issues related to gender disparity and biases in scholarly publishing, pay, and promotion can be, and should remain, the major concern of the entire academic community as well as the major scholarly societies. However, it was apparent that the numerous crises have deep roots in academia, and eradicating these serious problems and crises will take time and effort, often in short supply at far too many colleges and universities.

NOTES

1. C. P. Snow. The Two *Cultures* (Cambridge: Cambridge University Press, 1998). p. 4. This 1998 edition has an exceptional introduction by Stefan Collini.
2. Ibid., p. 9.
3. Ibid., p. 13.
4. Ibid., pp. 14–15.
5. Ibid., pp. 17–18.
6. Ibid., p. 22.
7. Ibid., pp. 61–62.
8. Ibid., p. 68.
9. Ibid., 99–100. Also see Lawrence M. Krauss. "An Update on C.P. Snow's 'Two Cultures';" https://www.scienceamerican.com/article/an-update-on-CP-snows-two-cultures. Academic Librarian. "The 'Crisis' in the Humanities;" https://blogs.princeton.edu/librarian/2010/11/the-crisis-in-the-humanities. Stanley Fish. "The Crisis in the Humanities Officially Arrives;" https://archive.nytimes.com/opinionator.blogs.nytimes.com/2010/10/11/the-crisis-of-the-humanities-officially-arrives. Timothy Aubry. "Humanities, Inc.," *American Studies 53*,4(2014): 5–29.
10. David Arndt. "The Two Cultures and the Crisis in the Humanities," https://files.eric.ed.gov/fulltext/EJ1098521.pdf.
11. Ibid.
12. Ibid. Also see Aden Barton. "Five Theses on the Humanities Crisis;" https://www.harvardcrimson.com/article/2022/12/1/barton-humanities-crisis. Derek Bok. *Attacking the Elites* (New Hanen: Yale University Press, 2024), pp. 48–166. Natalia Mayorga. "The 'Permanent Crisis' of the Humanities;" https://www.jamesmartin.center/2021/10/the=permanent-crisis-of-the-humanities. Dylan Ruediger. "The State of the Humanities: Notes from the National Humanities Alliance Annual Meeting;" https://sr.ithaka.org/blog/the-state-of-the-humanities.
13. J.H. Plumb. *Crisis in the Humanities* (Baltimore, MD: Penguin Books, 1964), pp. 7–8.

14. Ibid., p. 26.
15. Ibid. p. 44. Also see Adam Sitze, Austin Sarat, and Boris Wolfson. "The Humanities in Question;" *College Literature 42*, 2(Spring 2015): 191–220. Abraham Flexner. "The Usefulness of Useless Knowledge;" https://www.ias.edu/sites/default/files/library//UsefullHarpers.pdf. Steven Mintz. "The Humanities: A Status Report;" https://www.insidehighereducation.com/blogs/higher-ed-gamma/humanities-status-report. Aaron Hanlon. "The Humanities Are Facing a Credibility Crisis;" https://www.washingtonpost.com/outlook/2022/04/15/humanities-sciences-credibility-crisis-public-trust.
16. Roger Kimball. "'The Two Cultures' Today;" https://newcriterion.com/article/aoethe-two-cultures-today. Also see Jeffrey R. DiLeo. "The Rise of Corporate Literature: Crisis in the Humanities;" https://doi.org/10.1353/abr.2011.0086.
17. Ibid.
18. Stanley Fish. "The Crisis of the Humanities Officially Arrives;" https://archive.nytimes.com/opinionator.blogs.nytimes.com/2010/10/11/the-crisis-of-the-humanities-officially-arrives. Also see the American Academy of Arts and Sciences. "Higher Education;" https://www.amacad.org/humanities-indicators/higher-education.
19. Ibid. Also see Walter J. Ong. "Crisis and Understanding in the Humanities, *Daedalus 98*, 3 (Summer 1969): 617–640. " Palmer Rampell and Jordan Brower. "How Harold Bloom Misunderstood the Fall of the Humanities;" https://washingtonpost.com/outlook/2019/10/24/how-harold-bloom-misumderstood-fall-humanities.
20. Marjorie Perloff. "Crisis in the Humanities;" https://writing.upenn.edu/epc/authors/perloff/articles/crisis.html. Also see Geoffrey Galt Harpham. "Beneath and Beyond the 'Crisis in the Humanities'," New Literary History 36(2005): 21–36.
21. Ibid. Also see Ben Goldstein. "Decline of the Humanities: Where Does It STEM From?" https://journals.library.cornell.edu/index.php/ted/article/view/635/612.
22. Ernest Hemingway. The quote is from *The Sun Also Rises*. "How did you go bankrupt? Gradually, then suddenly."
23. Leonard Cassuto. *The Graduate School Mess: What Caused It and How We Can Fix It* (Cambridge: Harvard University Press, 2015). Also see Paul Jay. *The Humanities 'Crisis' and the Future of Literary Studies* (New York: Palgrave Macmillan, 2014). Julie R. Posselt. *Inside Graduate Admissions: Merit, Diversity, and Faculty Gatekeeping* (Cambridge: Harvard University Press, 2016). Karin Wulf. "Humanities and Graduate Education: The Crisis is Real, But Not New;" https://scholarlykitchen.sspnet.org/2022/04/29/humanities-and-graduate-education-the-crisis-is-rea;-but-not-new.

24. James Monk. "Who Are the Part-time Faculty? There's No Such Thing as a Typical Part-timer;" https://www.aaup.org/article/who-are-part-time-faculty#:~:text=That%20%E2%80%9Cpart%2Dtime%20faculty%20are,respect%20than%20full%2Dtime%20faculty. Also see Steven Hurlburt and Michael McGarrah. "The Shifting Academic Workforce: Where Are the Contingent Faculty?" https://www.air.org/sites/default/files/downloads/report/Shifting-Academic-Workforce November-2016.pdf. Patrick M. Rossol-Allison and Natalie J. Alleman Beyers. "The Role of Full-Time and Part-Time Faculty in Student Learning Outcomes;" https://files.eric.ed.gov/fulltext/ED531726.pdf.

25. The Hechinger Report. "Proof Points: 861 colleges and 9,499 Campuses Have Closed Since 2004;" https://hechingerreport.com/proof-points-861-colleges-and-0499-campuses-have-closed-down-since-2004. Hechinger's totals included public, private non-profit, and private for-profit colleges. Also see the American Academy of Arts and Sciences. "The Number of College Graduates in the Humanities Drops for the Eighth Consecutive year;" https://www.amacad.org/news/college-graduates-humanities-drops-eighth-consecutive-year. Best Colleges. "Closed Colleges: List, Statistics, and Major Closures;" https://www.bestcolleges.com/research/closed-colleges-list-statistics-major-closures. Best Colleges surveyed higher education between 2020 and 2024.

26. Christopher John Newfield. "The Humanities Crisis Is a Funding Crisis;" https://president.mla.hcommons.org/2022/08/10/the-humanities-crisis-is-a-funding-crisis.

27. College Art Association. "CAA News Today;' https://www.collegeart.org/news/2018/11/08/colleges-facing-cuts-to-arts-and-humanities.

28. Nick Anderson. "Marymount University Cuts English, Several Other Majors;" https://washingtonpost.com/education/2023/02/24/marymount-university-humanities-majors-eliminated.

29. Melissa Korn and Kris Maher. "University's Budget Woes Roil West Virginia," the Wall Street Journal, August 29, 2023, p. A5.

30. University of Arizona Library. "UA Library Budget;" https://lib.arizona.edu/about/organization/budget. Also see U.S. Department of Education, National Center for Educational Statistics. "Academic Libraries;" https://nces.ed.gov/pubs2004/2004317.pdf.

31. Anne Ford. "When Universities Cut, Libraries Bleed;" https://americanlibrariesmagazine.org/2018/11/01/when-universities-cut-libraries-bleed.

32. Ibid.

33. *Daily Record*. "Rutgers Should Restore Library Budget;" https://www.dailyrecord.com/story/opinion/letters/2014/11/01/rutgers-restore-library-budget/18258013.

34. Amy Res. "LJ's State of Academic Libraries Survey Reveals Challenges, Priorities;" https://www.libraryjournal.com/story/LJs-State-of-Academic-Libraries-Survey-Reveals-Challenges-Priorities. Also see Lisa Peet. "LJs College Student Library Usage Survey Reveals Positive Views, Inconsistent Engagement;" https://www.libraryjournal.com/story/ljs-college-student-library-survey-reveals-positive-views-inconsistent-engagement.

35. *Library Journal.* "College Student Library Usage Survey Report 2022;" https://www.libraryjournal.com/story/LJs-college=student-library-usage-survey-reveals-positive-views-inconsistent-engagements).

36. Association of College and Research Libraries (ACRL). "Top Trends in Academic Libraries;" file:///C:/Users/angre/Downloads/25483-50600-1-Sm.pdf; "2020 ACRL Academic Library Trends and Statistics Survey;" https://crin.acrl.org/index.php/crinnews/article/view/25402/33284; "2020 Top Trends in Academic Libraries;" https://crin.acrl.org/index.php/crinews/article/view/24478/32315; "Top Issues Facing Academic Libraries: A Report of the Focus on the Future Task Force;" https://crin.acrl.org/index.php/crinews/article/view/18396/20767.

37. Danielle Cooper, Catherine Bond Hill, and Roger C. Schoenfeld. "Aligning the Research Library to Organizational Strategy;" https://www.library-journal.com/story/The-New-Abnormal-Periodicals-Price-Survey-2021. Also see Patrick O'Donnell and Loraine Anderson. "The University Library: Places for Possibility," *New Review of Academic Librarianship 28,* 3(2022): 232–255.

38. The Federal Reserve Bank of St. Louis. "Economic Research;" https://research.stlouisfed.org/publications/page1-econ/2021/03/01/the-science-of-supply-and-demand. "The law of demand describes the behavior of buyers in markets. As the price (P) of a good or service rises, the quantity demanded (Q_D) of that good or service falls. Likewise, as the price of a good or service falls, the quantity demanded of that good or service rises. Consider your favorite snack food. A downward sloping demand curve indicates that as the price of the snack increases, you would be able and/or willing to buy a smaller amount. This relationship is demonstrated by the downward sloping demand curve in Figure 3. When the price increases from P_1 to P_2, the quantity demanded decreases from Q_1 to Q_2. Similarly, the law of supply describes the behavior of sellers in markets: As the price of a good or service rises, the quantity supplied of that good or service rises. Likewise, as the price of a good or service falls, the quantity supplied of that good or service falls. Therefore, as the price (as determined by the market) of your favorite snack rises, firms are willing to produce more units. This relationship is demonstrated by the graph of the upward sloping supply curve in Figure 4. When the price increases from P_1

to P_2, firms are willing to supply a greater quantity. That is, the quantity supplied increases from Q_1 to Q_2."

39. Alia Wong. "College Students Just Want Normal Libraries;" https://www.theatlantic.com/education/archive/2019/10/college-students-dont-want-fancy-libraries/599455.

40. Dan Cohen. "The Books of College Libraries Are Turning Into Wallpaper;" https://www.theatlantic.com/ideas/archive/2019/05/college-students-arent-checking-out-books/590305.

41. Ibid. Also see Gwen Evans and Roger C. Schoenfeld. "It's Not What Libraries Hold: It's Who Libraries Serve;" https://sr.ithaka.org/publications/its-not-what-libraries-hold-its-who-libraries-serve. Also see Jennifer K. Frederick and Christine Wolff-Eisenberg. "Ithaka S + R U.S. Library Survey 2019;" https://sr.ithaka.org/wp-content/uploads/2020/04/SR-Report-US-Library-directors-Survey-2019-040220.pdf.

42. Association of College and Research Libraries. "2021 ACRL Academic Library Trends and Statistics Survey;" https://crin.acrl.org/index.php/crinews/article/view/25850/33784.Also see David W. Lewis, Tina Baich, Kristi L. Palmer, and Willie M. Miller. "The Efficient Provision of Information Resources in Academic Libraries: Theory and Practice," Library Trends 70, 3(Winter 2022): 323–354. Also see Ioana G. Hulbert. "Ithaka S + R U.S> Library Survey 2022;" https://sr.ithaka.org/wp-content/uploads/2023/03/SR-Report-2022-US-Library-Director-Survey-03302023.pdf.

43. Paul N. Current and Matthew Nielsen. "On the Cost of Keeping A Book;" https://textlibris.lib.utexas.edu/wp-content/uploads/2018/08/CourantandNielsen.pdf.

44. Ibid.

45. University of Illinois. "University Library Collections: Library Administration;" https://www.library.illinois.edu/collections. The University of Illinois library "holds over 14,000,000 volume and 24 million other items, including electronic books, maps, slides, audio tapes, microforms, DVDs, videotapes, laser disks, and video games."

46. Laura Rise and Caroline Covington. "The Library Is Far From Obsolete. But This 'Temple of Learning' Must Constantly Adapt to Survive;" https://www.texasstandard.org/stories/libraries=are-far-from-obsolete-but-these-temples-of-learning-must-constantly-adapt-to-survive.

47. Michael Rubinkam. "Why University Libraries Are Tossing Millions of Books;"https://www.csmonitor.com/books/2018/0207/why-university-libraries-are-tossing-millions-of-books.

48. Mary E. Miller and Suzanne M. Ward. "Rightsizing Your Collection: Make the Academic Collection Management Process More Intentional and

User-Centric;" https://americanlibrariesmagazine.org/2022/05/02/rightsizing-your-collection. Also see Evan Ira Farber. "Books Not for College Libraries: A Singular Proposal;" https://www.ala.org/acrl/publications/whitepapers/nashville/farber.

49. Matthew J. Jabaily, James R. Rodgers, and Steven A. Knowlton. "Leveraging Use-By-Publication-Age Data in Serials Collection Decisions;" https://doi.org/10.5703/1288284316271. Also see Ye Mun, Heidi card, Kathleen McCormick, Kristy While, Tracy Ballack, and Robert Behary. "Rations for Evaluating Full-text Journal Article Access: A Quantitative Study;" https://doi.org/10.1080/0361526X.2022.2139331.

50. Preeti Kori, Bodian Li, Stefan McCabe, Jon Geen, David Lazer, Christopher R. Marsicano, Samuel V. Scarpino, and Alessandro Vespignani Preeti Kori, Bodian Li, Stefan McCabe, Jon Geen, David Lazer, Christopher R. Marsicano, Samuel V. Scarpino, and Alessandro Vespignani. "Higher Education Responses to Covid-19 in the United States: Evidence for the Impacts of University Policy;" https://journals.plos.org/digitalhealth/article?id=10.1371/journal.pdig.0000065.

51. Alan R. Hamlin and Steve T. Barney. "The Impact of Covid-19 on U.S. College Students, and How Educators Should Respond;" https://eric.ed.gov/?id=EJ1347721. Also see Jenny Lee, Matthew Solomon, Tej Stead, Beyan Kwon, and Latha Ganti. "Impact of Covid-19 on the Mental Health of U.S. College Students;" https://bmcpsychology.biomedcentral.com/articles;10.1186/s40359-021-00598-3. Kesong Hu, Kaylene Godfrey, Oiping Ren, Shenlian Wang, Xuemei Yang, and Oi Li. "The Impact of the Covid-19 Pandemic on College Students in USA: Two years Later;" https://doi.org/10.1016/j.psychres.2022.114685.

52. National Student Clearinghouse Research Center. "Stay Informed With the Latest Enrollment Information;" https://nscresearchcenter.org/stay-informed/?gad_source=1&gclid=Cj0KCQjw6auyBhDzARIsALIo6v_FAL58mWRt7xufuJmsswVs-zd4Wdb3omN5VRwOVVWSCEtKYBzOUsEaAgszEALw_wcB.

53. Phillip W. Magness. "The Brutalization of College Students During Lockdown;" https://www.aier.org/article/the-brutalization-of-college-students-during-lockdowns/?gad_source=1&gclid=Cj0KCQjw6auyBhDzARIsALIo6v9Ki0e8Ozd_u7vlBKWqkFuqfh25geNQRB1AyFPhsnF-8j94G5DEsZQaAlI4EALw_wcB.

54. Kesong Hu, Kaylene Godfrey, Qiping Ren, Shenlian Wang, Xuemei Yang, and Qi Li "The Impact of the Covid-19 Pandemic on College Students in the U.S.A.: Two Years Later;" https://doi.org/10.1016/j.psychres.2022.114685.

55. Senait Fisseha, Gita Sen, Tedros Adhanom Ghebreyesus, Winnie Byanyima, Debora Diniz, Henrieta H. Fore, Natalia Kanem, Ulrika Karlsson, Rajat, Khosla, Laura Laski, Dina Mired, Phumzile Mlambo-Ngcuka, Tlanemg Mofokeng, Geeta Rao Gupta, Achim Steiner, Michelle Remme, and Pascale Allotney. "Covid-19: The Turning Point for Gender Equality;" https://www.thelancet.com/pdfs/journals/lancet/PHSO140-6736 (21)01651-2.pdf.

56. David Fang, Sonia K. Kang, and Sarah Kaplan. "We Need to Make Sure Telecommuting Does Not Exacerbate Gender Disparity;" https://www.thelancet.com/pdfs/journals/lancet/PHSO140-6736(22)01211-9.pdf.

57. Giuliana Viglione. "Are Women Publishing Less During the Pandemic? Here's What the Data Say;" https://www.nature.com/articles/d41586-020-01294-9. Also see David J. Samuels and Dawn Langan Teele. "New Medium, Same Story? Gender Gaps in Book Publishing;" https://www.cambridge.org/journals/ps-political-science-and-politics/article/new-medium-same-story-genger-gaps-in-book-publishing/CCE2C49F2E79729A603770AB905E202B. Nicola Wilson, Claire Battershill, and Sophie Heywood (editors). *The Edinburgh Companion to Women in Publishing: 1900–2020* (Edinburgh, Scotland: Edinburgh University Press, 2004), pp. 641–723.

58. Anna Fazackerley. "Women's Research Plummets During Lockdown—But Articles From Men Increases;" https://www.theguardian.com/education/2020/may/12/womens-research-plummets-during-lockdown-but-articles-from-men-increases-increase. Also see Tatyana Deryugina, Olga Shurchkov, and Jenna E. Stearns. "Covid-19 Disruptions Disproportionately Affect Female Academics;" https://www.nber.org/papers/w28360. Jocalyn Clark. "How Pandemic Publishing Stuck a Blow to the Visibility of Women's Expertise;" https://www.bmj.com/content/381/bm.p788.

59. Kim Eckart. "Is There a Glass Ceiling in Academic Publishing?" https://phys.org/news/2018-03-glass-ceiling-academic-publishing.html. Also see Alesia Zuccala and Gemma Derrick. "When It Comes to Gender Inequality in Academia, We Know Much More Than Can Be Measured;" https://blogs.ise.ac.uk/impactofsocialsciences/2021/01/26/when-it-comes-to-gender-inequality-in-academic-we-know-more-than-what-can-be-measured. Jevin D. West, Jennifer Jacquet, Molly M. King, Shelley J. Correll, and carl T. Bergstrom. "The Role of Gender in Scholarly Authorship," *PLOS ONE 8*, 7(July 2013)/e66212.

60. Donna K. Ginther and Kathy J. Hayes. "Gender Differences in Salary and Promotion in the Humanities," *American Economic Review 89*, 2(May 1959): 397–402. Also see Isabelle Regner, Catherine Thinus-Blanc, Agnes Netter, Toni Schmader, and Pascal Huguet. "Committees With Implicit

Biases Promote Fewer Women When They Do Not Believe Gender Bias Exists;" https://www.nature.com/articles/s41562-019-0686-3.

61. The National Humanities Center. "100 Years and Counting: The Continuing Struggle for Gender Equality;' https://action.nationalhumanitiescenter.org/100-years-counting-continuing-struggle-gender-equality. Also see American Association of University Women. "Barriers and Bias: The Status of Women in Leadership;" https://www.aauw.org/aap/uploads/2020-03/Barriers-and-bias-nsa.pdf. Jocalyn Clark and Roopa Dhatt. "Backsliding in Gender Equality: A Reminder That Progress Is A Constant;" https://www.bmj.com/content/379/bmj.o2469. Youssouf Merouani and Faustine Perrin. "Gender and the Long-Run Development Process: A Survey of the Literature;" https://doi.org/10.1093/ereh/heac008.

62. Cary Wu. "The Gender Citation Gap: Approaches, Explanations, and Implications;" https://doi.org/10.1111/soc4.13189. Also see Unislawa M. Williams. "The Publication Gender Gap, Collaboration, and An Index of Inclusion for Scholarly Publishing Peer-Reviewed Research;" https://doi.org/10.1017/S10490965220000828.

63. Amanda Heidt. "Racial Inequalities in Journals Highlighted in Giant Study;" https://www.nature.com/articles/d41586-023-01457-4. Also see Hayk Amirkhanyan, Michel Krawczyk, and Marciej Wilamowski. "Do Male and Female Authors Employ Different Journal Choice Strategies?" https://doi.org/10.1007/s11192-023-04829-9.

64. Alexander Michael Petersen, Santo Fortunato, Raj K. Pan, Kimmon Kaski, Orion Penner, Armando Rungi, Massimo Riccaboni, H. Eugene Stanley, and Fabio Pammolli. "Reputation and Impact in Academic Careers;" https://www.pnas.ord/doi/full/10.1073/pnas.1323111111.

65. John M. Herbert. "Tackling Pedigree Bias in Hiring;" https://www.insidehighered.com/opinion/views/2023/09/27/tackling-pedigree-bias-tenure-track-hiring-opinion.

66. K. Hunter Wapman, Sam Zhang, Aaron Clauset, and Daniel B. Larremore. "Quantifying Hierarchy and Dynamics in U.S. Faculty Hiring and Retention;" https://www.nature.com/articles/s41586-022-05222-x. Also see London School of Economics. "Why Are Women Cited Less Than Men?" https://blogs.ise.ac.uk/impactofsocialsciences/2024-03/25/why-are-women-cited-less-than-men.

67. Ryan Quinn. "Faculty Gender Imbalances Yield Biased Student Ratings;" https://www.insidehighered.com/news/2023/01/25/study-student-evaluation-bias-gender-lopsided-departments. Also see Oriana R. Aragon, Evava S. Pietri, and Brian A. Powell. "Gender Bias in Teaching Evaluations: The Casual Role of Department Gender Composition;" https://www.pnas.org/doi/10.1073/pnas.2118466120.

68. Colleen Flaherty. "Ratings and Gender Bias Over Time;" https://www.insidehighered.com/news/2022/10/31/ratings-and-bias-against-women0over-time.
69. American Alliance of Museums (AAM). "Museum Facts and Data;" https://www.aam-us.org/programs/about-museums/museums-facts-data.
70. The Metropolitan Museum of Art. "Building and Caring for the Met Collection;"https://www.metmuseum.org/articles/building-and-caring-for-the-met-collection.

CHAPTER 5

Intellectual Property Issues on the Humanities and Scholarly Publishing: 2000–2024

Abstract The legal basis in the United States for intellectual property (IP) is the U.S. Constitution in Article 1 § 8. However, it was the responsibility of the U.S. Congress to pass laws regarding patents, trademarks, and copyrights, issues of great importance to humanities scholars and authors. This chapter outlines briefly the terms and conditions of patents and trademarks. However, there is a detailed analysis of some key provisions of the U.S. Copyright Law (17 U.S.C.), a list and description of certain important copyright cases, and a detailed analysis of the important Sci-Hub copyright infringement case (in the Southern District of New York) regarding the illegal acquisition and posting for free of more than 65 million journal articles (possibly every scholarly article published since January 1665) and more than two million books.

Keywords Intellectual property • U.S. Copyright law • Copyrights • Trademarks • Patents • Copyright infringement • USPTO

© The Author(s), under exclusive license to Springer Nature Switzerland AG 2024
A. N. Greco, *Scholarly Publishing in the Humanities, 2000–2024*, Marketing and Communication in Higher Education, https://doi.org/10.1007/978-3-031-66170-9_5

INTELLECTUAL PROPERTY: TRADEMARKS, TRADE SECRETS, PATENTS, AND COPYRIGHTS: AN INTRODUCTION

"Intellectual property [IP] consists of patents, trademarks, and copyright, which can be products or intangibles owned and legally protected by a company, an individual (s), or an estate from use or implementation without consent."[1]

The legal foundation for intellectual property in the United States is Article 1 § 8 of the U.S. Constitution.[2] This critically important section states that "the Congress shall have power to... promote the progress of science and useful arts, by securing for limited times to authors and inventors the exclusive right to their respective writings and discoveries."[3]

The First Amendment of the U.S. Constitution, which is part of the "Bill of Rights," does not address specifically intellectual property; however, it does deal with ideas and concepts of great importance to authors and scholarly book and journal publishers. "Congress shall make no law respecting an establishment of religion, or prohibiting the free exercise thereof; or abridging the freedom of speech, or of the press; or the right of the people peaceably to assemble, and to petition the government for a redress of grievances."[4]

Both Article 1 § 8 and the First Amendment are rather brief. So, it was up to the Congress of the United States to draft and pass laws designed specifically to offer protection for patents, trademarks, and copyrights. Copyrights and trademarks are of the greatest importance to authors and scholarly book and journal publishers since the laws provide legal protection for the author's work as well as the right of a publisher to print and distribute the author's work. A number of book publishers held various patents (e.g., Elsevier).

PATENTS

The United States Patent and Trademark Office (USPTO)

is an agency of the U.S. Department of Commerce (Commerce). The role of the USPTO is to grant patents for the protection of inventions and to register trademarks. It serves the interests of inventors and businesses with respect to their inventions and corporate products, and service identifications. It also advises and assists the President of the United States, the

Secretary of Commerce, the bureaus and offices of the Department of Commerce, and other agencies of the government in matters involving all domestic and global aspects of 'intellectual property.' Through the preservation, classification, and dissemination of patent information, the Office promotes the industrial and technological progress of the nation and strengthens the economy. In discharging its patent related duties, the USPTO examines applications and grants patents on inventions when applicants are entitled to them; it publishes and disseminates patent information, records assignments of patents, maintains search files of U.S. and foreign patents, and maintains a search room for public use in examining issued patents and records. The Office supplies copies of patents and official records to the public. It provides training to practitioners as to requirements of the patent statutes and regulations, and it publishes the Manual of Patent Examining Procedure to elucidate these. Similar functions are performed relating to trademarks. By protecting intellectual endeavors and encouraging technological progress, the USPTO seeks to preserve the United States' technological edge, which is key to our current and future competitiveness. The USPTO also disseminates patent and trademark information that promotes an understanding of intellectual property protection and facilitates the development and sharing of new technologies worldwide.[5]

USPTO defines a patent as follows.

A patent for an invention is the grant of a property right to the inventor, issued by the United States Patent and Trademark Office. Generally, the term of a new patent is 20 years from the date on which the application for the patent was filed in the United States or, in special cases, from the date an earlier related application was filed, subject to the payment of maintenance fees. U.S. patent grants are effective only within the United States, U.S. territories, and U.S. possessions. Under certain circumstances, patent term extensions or adjustments may be available. The right conferred by the patent grant is, in the language of the statute and of the grant itself, 'the right to exclude others from making, using, offering for sale, or selling' the invention in the United States or 'importing' the invention into the United States. What is granted is not the right to make, use, offer for sale, sell or import, but the right to exclude others from making, using, offering for sale, selling or importing the invention. Once a patent is issued, the patentee must enforce the patent without aid of the USPTO.

"There are three types of patents:

1) Utility patents may be granted to anyone who invents or discovers any new and useful process, machine, article of manufacture, or composition of matter, or any new and useful improvement thereof;

2) Design patents may be granted to anyone who invents a new, original, and ornamental design for an article of manufacture; and

3) Plant patents may be granted to anyone who invents or discovers and asexually reproduces any distinct and new variety of plant."[6]

USPTO also has information about U.S. Patent Laws.

Under this [the U.S. Constitution] power, Congress has from time to time enacted various laws relating to patents. The first patent law was enacted in 1790. The patent laws underwent a general revision which was enacted July 19, 1952, and which came into effect January 1, 1953. It is codified in Title 35, United States Code. Additionally, on November 29, 1999, Congress enacted the American Inventors Protection Act of 1999 (AIPA), which further revised the patent laws. See Public Law 106-113, 113 Stat. 1501 (1999). The patent law specifies the subject matter for which a patent may be obtained and the conditions for patentability. The law establishes the United States Patent and Trademark Office to administer the law relating to the granting of patents and contains various other provisions relating to patents.[7]

TRADEMARKS

USPTO defines a trademark as "a brand name. A trademark or service mark includes any word, name, symbol, device, or any combination, used or intended to be used to identify and distinguish the goods/services of one seller or provider from those of others, and to indicate the source of the goods/services."[8]

USPTO also provides a series of recommendations for any company, individual, or estate interested in maintaining legal control over a trademark. "Although federal registration of a mark is not mandatory, it has several advantages, including notice to the public of the registrant's claim of ownership of the mark, legal presumption of ownership nationwide, and exclusive right to use the mark on or in connection with the goods/services listed in the registration... An important consideration is the depiction of your mark. Every application must include a clear representation of the mark you want to register. We use this representation to file the mark in the USPTO search records and to print the mark in the Official

Gazette (OG) and on the registration certificate. The OG, a weekly online publication, gives notice to the public that the USPTO plans to issue a registration... Once you have chosen your mark, you must also be able to identify the goods and/or services to which the mark will apply, clearly and precisely. The identification of goods and/or services must be specific enough to identify the nature of the goods and/or services. The level of specificity depends on the type of goods and/or services."[9]

"While a patent is for a maximum period of time (i.e., 20 years), trademarks are registered for a period of 10 years, with 10 year renewal terms. So, as long as an individual or a company defends the trademarks and complies with any USPTO reporting requirement(s), there is no limit to the number of times a trademark can be renewed."[10]

While most book or journal publishing firms do not have a patent(s), the reverse is true regarding trademarks. Large and small trade houses have registered trademarks to differentiate a firm (e.g., Macmillan), an imprint (e.g., Henry Holt & Co.), or a book series (e.g., the Macmillan English Series) in what is a crowded marketplace. This requires the firm to monitor constantly and carefully address any possible infringement(s), which in the age of the internet and book and journal pirates remains a major concern.

COPYRIGHTS

As with patents and trademarks, the Congress had to create a copyright law. While there was copyright protection in the American colonies before 1776, the prevailing law was from England and its copyright law. When the newly created U.S. government had to draft a copyright law, America looked to England for guidance since they were familiar with the English copyright law of 1710.

In 1790 the Congress passed the country's first copyright law, based to a significant degree on England's 1710 law. This rather brief U.S. copyright law stipulated that copyright protection would last for 14 years, with another 14-year renewal (for a maximum total of 28 years), the basic terms of England's copyright law. The law contained provisions for prosecuting copyright infringers and deposit requirements.[11]

Copyright law revisions require extensive analyses; and the U.S. Congress has a history of deliberate discussions before making any substantive changes. It took 41 years before any changes were made in copyright law. In 1831, the United States adopted a new copyright law, again heavily influenced by England's changes in its copyright law. The term of protection was extended for 28 years, with the option to request an additional 14 years (for a total of 42 years).[12] Because of political events that engulfed the nation before (e.g., the 1850s) and during the Civil War (e.g., 1861–1865), Congress was compelled to wait 39 years before having the opportunity to draft new legislation. "The Copyright Act of 1870" did not extend copyright protection beyond the 42 year limit; but the law placed within the Library of Congress all copyright operations. In addition, revised registration and deposit requirements were added."[13] After yet another 39 years, Congress again revisited the copyright law in 1909, and Congress extended the term of copyright protection from 42 years to 56 years. Other key provision of the 1909 law clarified issues related to copyright dating and subject matter concerns.[14]

The years after 1909 were filled with internal turmoil (i.e., the need to address important domestic regulatory issues), and the outbreak of and impact of World War I in Europe (1914) on America. The United States entered the war in 1917. Economic booms in the 1920s were offset by the draconian impact of the Great Depression (which started in October 1929). So, the Congress was preoccupied with the various New Deal strategies to combat steep business declines, the rising unemployment rate, and social unrest. The outbreak of World II in Europe on September 1, 1939, and America's entry into the war on December 7, 1941, pushed aside any discussions about changes in copyrights. After the end of World War II, the Congress in 1947 created a unified copyright law known as 17 U.S.C.[15]

Peacetime prosperity after 1947 and the Bicentennial of the United States in 1976 prompted the Congress to evaluate again a series of needed changes in the copyright law in order to comply with the provisions of the Berne Convention (discussed below in the material about 17 U.S.C. §101). The major changes in copyright law were significant: the term of copyright protection was extended to the life of the author and 50 years after the death of the author. Works with multiple authors were addressed, and the 50 years limit was extended to the last surviving author; and corporate ownership of a copyright was extended to 75 years after the initial granting of copyright protection. Works that received copyright protection before January 1, 1978, received a term of 47 years for a maximum term of 75 years.[16]

The Congress updated the copyright law with the controversial "Copyright Term Extension Act of 1998," which is often called the

"Mickey Mouse Protection Act" because of the unusual extension of the Walt Disney's cartoon character Mickey Mouse (due to extensive lobbying by the Walt Disney Company).[17] However, this act also addressed substantive matters related to an extension of copyright protection for the life of the author and 70 years after the death of the author; and the revision contained provisions for multiple authors followed the 1976 guidelines regarding the 70-year provision after the death of the last surviving author. Some other key provisions included the following: all corporate copyrights were extended to 120 years after the creation of the work or 95 years after the work's original publication, and all works published prior to January 1, 1978, were extended to 95 years.[18] Congress also passed the 1998 "Digital Millennium Copyright Act," which addressed infringement on what was at that time the "new" internet as well as language regarding digital rights managements systems and procedures.[19]

The entire 17 U.S.C. is a very long 484-page document, and it is available free online. However, anyone who wants to become a published author, or, for that matter, anyone working in a scholarly book or scholarly journal firm would find a basic understanding of the terms and conditions stipulated in 17 U.S.C. of great importance. For example, a number of the sections listed below were referenced specifically in the Sci-Hub case. While it would be difficult to mention more than just a few of the law's key provisions of substantive importance to authors and scholarly publishers, the following provides a brief outline of some of the important provisions of the U.S. Copyright Law.

- **17 U.S.C §101** · "Definitions: Except as otherwise provided in this title, as used in this title, the following terms and their variant forms mean the following: An 'anonymous work' is a work on the copies or phonorecords of which no natural person is identified as author. An 'architectural work' is the design of a building as embodied in any tangible medium of expression, including a building, architectural plans, or drawings. The work includes the overall form as well as the arrangement and composition of spaces and elements in the design, but does not include individual standard features. 'Audiovisual works' are works that consist of a series of related images which are intrinsically intended to be shown by the use of machines or devices such as projectors, viewers, or electronic equipment, together with accompanying sounds, if any, regardless of the nature of the material objects, such as films or tapes, in which the works are embodied. The

'Berne Convention' is the Convention for the Protection of Literary and Artistic Works, signed at Berne, Switzerland, on September 9, 1886, and all acts, protocols, and revisions thereto. The 'best edition' of a work is the edition, published in the United States at any time before the date of deposit, that the Library of Congress determines to be most suitable for its purposes. A person's 'children' are that person's immediate offspring, whether legitimate or not, and any children legally adopted by that person. A 'collective work' is a work, such as a periodical issue, anthology, or encyclopedia, in which a number of contributions, constituting separate and independent works in themselves, are assembled into a collective whole. A 'compilation' is a work formed by the collection and assembling of preexisting materials or of data that are selected, coordinated, or arranged in such a way that the resulting work as a whole constitutes an original work of authorship. The term 'compilation' includes collective works. A 'computer program' is a set of statements or instructions to be used directly or indirectly in a computer in order to bring about a certain result. 'Copies' are material objects, other than phonorecords, in which a work is fixed by any method now known or later developed, and from which the work can be perceived, reproduced, or otherwise communicated, either directly or with the aid of a machine or device. The term 'copies' includes the material object, other than a phonorecord, in which the work is first fixed. 'Copyright owner,' with respect to any one of the exclusive rights comprised in a copyright, refers to the owner of that particular right... A work is 'created' when it is fixed in a copy or phonorecord for the first time; where a work is prepared over a period of time, the portion of it that has been fixed at any particular time constitutes the work as of that time, and where the work has been prepared in different versions, each version constitutes a separate work... A work consisting of editorial revisions, annotations, elaborations, or other modifications, which, as a whole, represents an original work of authorship, is a 'derivative work...' A work is 'fixed' in a tangible medium of expression when its embodiment in a copy or phonorecord, by or under the authority of the author, is sufficiently permanent or stable to permit it to be perceived, reproduced, or otherwise communicated for a period of more than transitory duration... An 'international agreement' is—(1) the Universal Copyright Convention; (2) the

Geneva Phonograms Convention; (3) the Berne Convention; (4) the WTO Agreement; (5) the WIPO Copyright Treaty;13 (6) the WIPO Performances and Phonograms Treaty;14 and (7) any other copyright treaty to which the United States is a party... A 'joint work' is a work prepared by two or more authors with the intention that their contributions be merged into inseparable or interdependent parts of a unitary whole. 'Literary works' are works, other than audiovisual works, expressed in words, numbers, or other verbal or numerical symbols or indicia, regardless of the nature of the material objects, such as books, periodicals, manuscripts, phonorecords, film, tapes, disks, or cards, in which they are embodied... The offering to distribute copies or phonorecords to a group of persons for purposes of further distribution, public performance, or public display, constitutes publication... 'Registration,' for purposes of sections 205(c) (2), 405, 406, 410(d), 411, 412, and 506(e), means a registration of a claim in the original or the renewed and extended term of copyright... For purposes of section 411, a work is a 'United States work' only if—(1) in the case of a published work, the work is first published—(A) in the United States; (B) simultaneously in the United States and another treaty party or parties, whose law grants a term of copyright protection that is the same as or longer than the term provided in the United States; (C) simultaneously in the United States and a foreign nation that is not a treaty party; or (D) in a foreign nation that is not a treaty party, and all of the authors of the work are nationals, domiciliaries, or habitual residents of, or in the case of an audiovisual work legal entities with headquarters in, the United States; (2) in the case of an unpublished work, all the authors of the work are nationals, domiciliaries, or habitual residents of the United States, or, in the case of an unpublished audiovisual work, all the authors are legal entities with headquarters in the United States... A 'useful article' is an article having an intrinsic utilitarian function that is not merely to portray the appearance of the article or to convey information. An article that is normally a part of a useful article is considered a 'useful article'... A 'work of the United States Government' is a work prepared by an officer or employee of the United States Government as part of that person's official duties. A 'work made for hire' is—(1) a work prepared by an employee within the scope of his or her employment; or (2) a work specially ordered or commissioned for use as a contribution to a collective work... if the parties expressly agree in a written instrument signed by them that the work shall be considered a work made for hire."[20]

- **17 U.S.C. § 501 · Infringement of Copyright**

"Anyone who violates any of the exclusive rights of the copyright owner as provided by sections 106 through 122 or of the author as provided in section 106A(a), or who imports copies or phonorecords into the United States in violation of section 602, is an infringer of the copyright or right of the author, as the case may be...The legal or beneficial owner of an exclusive right under a copyright is entitled, subject to the requirements of section 411, to institute an action for any infringement of that particular right committed while he or she is the owner of it."[21]

- **17 U.S.C. § 502 · Remedies for Infringement: Injunctions**

Any court having jurisdiction of a civil action arising under this title may, subject to the provisions of section 1498 of title 28, grant temporary and final injunctions on such terms as it may deem reasonable to prevent or restrain infringement of a copyright."[22]

- **17 U.S.C. § 506 · Criminal Offenses**

"Criminal Infringement:—In general any person who willfully infringes a copyright shall be punished as provided under section 2319 of title 18, if the infringement was committed—for purposes of commercial advantage or private financial gain; by the reproduction or distribution, including by electronic means, during any 180-day period, of 1 or more copies or phonorecords of 1 or more copyrighted works, which have a total retail value of more than $1,000."[23]

- **17 U.S.C. § 107 · Limitations on Exclusive Rights: Fair Use**

"In determining whether the use made of a work in any particular case is a fair use the factors to be considered shall include—the purpose and character of the use, including whether such use is of a commercial nature or is for nonprofit educational purposes; the nature of the copyrighted work; the amount and substantiality of the portion used in relation to the copyrighted work as a whole; and the effect of the use upon the potential market for or value of the copyrighted work... The fact that a work is unpublished shall not itself bar a finding of fair use if such finding is made upon consideration of all the above factors."[24]

IMPORTANT COPYRIGHT CASES

Companies, individuals, or estates are very concerned about protecting intellectual rights. An interesting example is the Agatha Christie Limited estate. This estate controls more than 80 of her novels and short stories, 19 plays, and about 40 films; the estimates of the value of the Christie estate is in the millions of dollars. It has been estimated that only the Bible and Shakespeare have sold more books than Agatha Christie. Clearly, this literary estate is merely one of many others. For example, Robert Ludlum died in 2001; and his estate controls his 27 novels that have sold between 300 million and 500 million copies.

So, a literary estate must be diligent when it comes to identifying and protecting intellectual properties because IP holds such high value in today's increasingly knowledge-based economy. And extracting value from IP and preventing others from deriving value through piracy or infringement from IP is an important responsibility for a company, individual, or an estate.

While intellectual property is exceptionally valuable, many forms of IP cannot be listed on a balance sheet as assets; but, in many instances, the value of such IP tends to be reflected in the price of the stock. Consequently, management's ability to manage IP and turn a profit can be critical to a company, an individual, or an estate.

Since 1998, the Supreme Court of the United States has rendered decisions on 16 major copyright cases.[25] The important court cases include *Quality King Distributors v. L'anza Research Inter'l Inc.*, 523 U.S., (the first sale doctrine is of great importance to authors and publishers; see the Kirtsaeng case below); *Feltner v. Columbia Pictures Television, Inc.*, 523 U.S. 340, (the court addressed the right to a jury trial in a copyright infringement case); *The New York Times Co. v. Tasini*, 533 U.S. 483, (the journalist Tasini did not grant electronic republication rights for collective work); *Eldred v. Ashcroft*, 537 U.S. 186, (pertained to the duration of copyright); *Metro-Goldwyn-Mayer v. Grokster*, 545 U.S. 913, (an important copyright infringement decision); *Reed Elsevier v. Muchnick*, 559 U.S. 154, (another important copyright infringement case); *Golan v. Holder*, 565 U.S. 302, (concerned copyright in a public domain case); and *Kirtsaeng v. John Wiley & Sons, Inc.*, 568 U.S. 519, (this is the most important first sale copyright case since the *Bobbs-Merrill v. Strauss* 210 U.S. 339 case in 1908; the Court voted that the first sale doctrine applies to copyrighted works made lawfully overseas.

The entire scholarly publishing community, especially the Association of American Publishers (AAP), has been active in informing the Congress about the excessive piracy, infringement of IP, and the need for updates and changes in 17 U.S.C. After all, the Congress has not passed any significant revisions in this century to the copyright laws in spite of transformative changes in the channels of distribution because of the wide-spread acceptance and use of the internet, laptops and tablets, the digital posting of content online, etc.

The diverse members of the copyright community, especially large corporations, have shown great interest in copyright revisions; unfortunately, the Congress has not. It is important for authors and scholarly publishers to make the Congress aware of the need to support changes in the U.S. Copyright Law in light of the substantive developments in the way scholarly books and journals are preserved and/or transmitted in what is a global internet;[26] and, also of importance, is the need to support changes in the U.S. Copyright Office.[27]

Hope springs eternal; however, it was obvious in the Sci-Hub case, one of the most important copyright infringement case in the United States in decades, that intellectual property thieves and hackers have stolen and posted on the internet's dark web more than 65 million scholarly journal articles and more than two million books. The Sci-Hub case, held in the Southern District of New York (SDNY), involved scholarly book and journal publisher Elsevier Inc., Elsevier B.V., and Elsevier Ltd., the plaintiffs, against www.sci-hub.com, The Library Genesis Project, d/b/a/LIBGEN. org, Alexandra Elbakyan, and John Does 1-99, the defendants, of "distributing works to which Elsevier owns the copyright."[28]

The Federal Judge, Robert W. Sweet reviewed all of the facts and exhibits and information about the case, and he ruled as follows. "Elsevier has established that the Defendants have reproduced and distributed its copyrighted works, in violation of the exclusive rights established by 17 U.S.C. § 106... In order to prevail on a claim for infringement of copyright, 'two elements must be proven: (1) ownership of a valid copyright, and (2) copying of constituent elements of the work that are original'... Elsevier has made a substantial evidentiary showing, documenting the manner in which the Defendants access its ScienceDirect database of scientific literature and post copyrighted material on their own websites free of charge. According to Elsevier, the Defendants gain access to

ScienceDirect by using credentials fraudulently obtained from educational institutions, including educational institutions located in the Southern District of New York, which are granted legitimate access to ScienceDirect."[29]

Judge Sweet's conclusion stated that

> for the reasons set forth above, the motion for a preliminary injunction is granted. It is hereby ordered that: 1. The Defendants, their officers, directors, principals, agents, servants, employees, successors and assigns, and all persons and entities in active concert or participation with them, are hereby temporarily restrained from unlawful access to, use, reproduction, and/or distribution of Elsevier's copyrighted works and from assisting, aiding, or abetting any other person or business entity in engaging in unlawful access to, use, reproduction, and/or distribution of Elsevier's copyrighted works; 2. Upon the Plaintiffs' request, those organizations which have registered Defendants' domain names on behalf of Defendants shall disclose immediately to the Plaintiffs all information in their possession concerning the identity of the operator or registrant of such domain names and of any bank accounts or financial accounts owned or used by such operator or registrant; 3. Defendants shall not transfer ownership of the Defendants' websites during the pendency of this Action, or until further Order of the Court; 4. The TLD Registries for the Defendants' websites, or their administrators, shall place the domain names on registryHold/serverHold as well as serverUpdate, serverDelete, and serverTransfer prohibited statuses, until further Order of the Court; 5. The Defendants shall preserve copies of all computer files relating to the use of the websites and shall take all necessary steps to retrieve computer files relating to the use of the websites that may have been deleted before entry of this Order; and 6. That security in the amount of $5,000 be posted by the Plaintiffs within one week of the entry of this Order.[30]

Unfortunately, while Elsevier won in the SDNY, Sci-Hub's millions of journal articles and millions of books continued to be available for free on numerous mirror websites in various foreign locations, and their pernicious endeavor was copied by several other pirate websites. This theft by Sci-Hub deprived authors of their rightful legal protection and income, and scholarly publishers, in addition to Elsevier, lost millions of dollars because of Sci-Hub and other pirate websites.[31]

However, Anna's Archive is one of the biggest pirate websites in the world. They announced on their website that it is "the largest truly open library in human history. We mirror Sci-Hub and LIBGEN. We scrape and open source Z-lib and DuXiu, and more; 30,550,667 books 100,357,162 [scholarly journal] papers—preserved forever, All our code and data are completely open source... To increase the resiliency of Anna's Archive, we're looking for volunteers to run mirrors [web sites]... If you run a high-risk anonymous payment processor, please contact us. We are also looking for people to place tasteful small ads. All proceeds go to our preservation efforts."[32] It is rather ironic that pirates who violated the Copyright Law of the United States, and posted illegally millions of copyrighted journals and books are eager to participate and profit, on their terms, in a paid advertising system.

Conclusion

In reality, if nothing is done to attack and defeat the IP pirates and the websites posting illegally copyrighted IP content, all authors and scholarly publishers, and specifically scholars and authors in the humanities and other academic fields, will continue to sustain financial losses.

Notes

1. World Intellectual Property Alliance. "What Is Intellectual Property?". https://www.wipo.int/about-ip/en/. Also see Organization for Economic Co-operation and Development (OECD). "Intellectual Property Rights," https://stats.oecd.org/glossary/detail.asp?ID=3236. Adrian Johns. *Piracy: The Intellectual Property Wars From Gutenberg to Gates* (Chicago: University of Chicago Press, 2011), 6, 287–289, 497–498, 515–518. Aaron Barlow, The Limits of Ownership in the United States, in *Cultures of Copyright*, eds. Danielle Nicole Devos and Martine Courant Rite (New York: Peter Lang, 2015),13–25.
2. U.S. Constitution, http://www.archives.gov/exhibits/charters/constitution_transcript.html.
3. U.S. Constitution. Article 1 §8, https://www.senate.gov/civics/constitution_item/constitution.htm. Article 1 §8 forms the legal foundation for copyrights, patents, and trademarks. Also see William S. Strong, *The Copyright Book: A Practical Guide, 6th ed.* (Cambridge, MA.: MIT Press, 2014), 1–46, 47–76, 227–272.
4. The First Amendment, https://www.senate.gov/civics/constitution_item/constitution.htm.

5. United States Patent and Trademark Office (USPTO). "General Information Concerning Patents," https://www.uspto.gov/patents-getting-started/general-information-concerning-patents#heading-2.
6. Ibid.
7. United States Government Printing Office (GPO). U.S.C. Title 35 Patents, https://www.govinfo.gov/content/pkg/USCODE-2011-title35/html/USCODE-2011-title35.htm; and GPO. Public Law 106–113, 113 Stat. 1501 (1999). https://www.govinfo.gov/content/pkg/PLAW-106pub l113/html/PLAW-106publ113.htm. Also see Leila Tahmooresnejad and Catherine Beaudry. "Do Patents of Academic Funded Researchers Enjoy a Longer Life? A Study of Patent Renewal Decisions," https://doi.org/10.1371/journal.pone.0202643; https://journals.plos.org/plosone/article?id=10.1371/journal.pone.0202643. Patrick Boucher. "Recent Developments in U.S. Patent Law," *Physics Today 65*, 1 (2012); https://physicstoday.scitation.org/doi/full/10.1063/PT.3.1397
8. United States Patent and Trademark Office (USPTO). Trademark Basics, https://www.uspto.gov/trademarks-getting-started/trademark-basics.
9. Ibid.
10. Ibid. Also see United States Trademark Law. U.S.C. 15 §1127, https://www.uspto.gov/sites/default/files/trademarks/law/Trademark_Statutes.pdf. Also see USGPO. U.S.C. 15 §1127 https://www.govinfo.gov/app/details/USCODE-2011-title15/USCODE-2011-title15-chap22-subchapIII-sec1127. Ross Housewright. "Early Development of American Trademark Law," https://www.ischool.berkeley.edu/sites/default/files/Ross%20Housewright%20TM%20Paper%20-%20FINAL.pdf. Rebecca Tushnet. "Registering Disagreement: Registration in Modern American Trademark Law," http://harvardlawreview.org/wp-content/uploads/2017/01/867-941-Online-updated.pdf.
11. U.S. Copyright Act of 1790, 1 Statutes At Large, 124; https://copyright.gov/about/1790-copyright-act.html. Also see Roger Schechter, *Intellectual Property: The Law of Copyrights, Patents, and Trademarks* (St Paul, MN: West Academic Publishing, 2008), 5–81; Sheldon W. Halpern, *Copyright Law: Protection of Original Expression* (Durham, NC: Carolina Academic Press, 2010), 10–71.
12. U.S. Copyright Office. Circular 1a: "United States Copyright Office: A Brief Introduction and History"; at www.copyright.goc/circs/circ1a.html.
13. U.S. Copyright Office. Circular 1a: "United States Copyright Office: A Brief Introduction and History"; at www.copyright.goc/circs/circ1a.html
14. Ibid.
15. A complete copy of 17 U.S.C. is available at https://www.copyright.gov/title17; and it contains the text of Title 17 of the United States Code including all amendments enacted by Congress. The United States copy-

right law is contained in chapters 1 through 8 and 10 through 12 of Title 17 of the United States Code (17 U.S.C.). Also see Bennett Cerf. *At Random: The Reminiscences of Bennett Cerf* (New York: Random House, 2002), pp. 195–230. William E. Leuchtenberg. *Franklin D. Roosevelt and the New Deal: 1932–1940* (New York: HarperCollins, 2009), pp. 1–18, 118–142, 197–230. Arthur M. Schlesinger. *The Age of Roosevelt: The Coming of the New Deal* (Boston: Houghton Mifflin Company, 1959), pp. 87–178.

16. Title 17 of the United States Code. Also see The Berne Convention for the Protection of Literary and Artistic Works; http://www.wipo.int/treaties/en/ip/berne/summary/berne.html. WIPO (the World Intellectual Property Organizations) stated that "The Berne Convention deals with the protection of works and the rights of their authors. It is based on **three basic principles** and contains a series of provisions determining the **minimum protection** to be granted, as well as special provisions available to **developing countries** that want to make use of them." Albert N. Greco, *The Economics of the Publishing and Information Industries* (New York: Routledge, 2015), 259–287. A few very useful websites with interesting information about specialized copyright issues include: Copyright Clearance Center www.copyright.com; Music: ASCAP www.ascap.com/licensing; BMI www.bmi.com/licensing; SESAC www.sesac.com/licensing/obtainlicense.aspx; Photos: Getty Images www.gettyimages.com; Corbis Images www.corbisimages.com

17. This law has been called the "Mickey Mouse Protection Act" since it extended the copyright protection for the cartoon character Mickey Mouse. See Lawrence Lessing, "Copyright's First Amendment," *UCLA Law Review 48 (2001):* 1057–1065.

18. Pub. L. 94-533; 17 U.S.C §§ 101–810; available at http://legislink.org/us/pl+94-553; 17 U.S.C §§ 101–81. Also see Cornell University Law School. "Copyright: Overview"; available at: https://www.law.cornell.edu/wex/copyright; and Cornell University Law School. "Direct Infringement"; available at: https://www.law.cornell.edu/wex/direct_infringement; and Cornell University Law School. "Secondary Liability;" available at: https://www.cornell.edu/wex/secondary_liability; and Cornell University Law School. "Contributory Infringement;" available at: https://www.cornell.edu/wex/contributory_infringement; and The Intellectual Trademark Association, "Combating Contributory Infringement on the Internet," *INTA Bulletin 69,* 9(May 1, 2014): 1–5; and U.S. Copyright Office, www.copyright.gov; for circulars at: www.copyright.gov/circs.

19. Pub. L., 105–298; 122 Stat.2827; 17 U.S.C. §§108 203(a), 301(c), 302, 303, 304(c)(2); available at: htttp://legislink.org/us/pl-105-298. Also see "Frequently Asked Questions About Copyright," https://www.copyright.gov/help/faq/index.html. Also see U.S. Copyright Office. Copyright Basics, https://www.copyright.gov/circs/circ01.pdf.
20. 17 U.S. C. §501; https://www.copyright.gov/title17.
21. 17 U.S. C. §501; https://www.copyright.gov/title17.
22. 17 U.S. C. §502; https://www.copyright.gov/title17.
23. 17 U.S.C. §506; https://www.copyright.gov/title17.
24. 17 U.S. C. §107; https://www.copyright.gov/title17.
25. Supreme Court of the United States major decisions about major copyright cases include: (a) *Quality King Distributors v. L'anza Research Inter'l Inc.*, 523 U.S.135, https://supreme.justia.com/cases/federal/us/523/135 [the first sale doctrine]; (b) *Feltner v. Columbia Pictures Television, Inc.*, 523 U.S. 340, https://supreme.justia.com/cases/federal/us/523/340; [right to a jury trial in a copyright infringement case]; (c) *New York Times Co. v. Tasini*, 533 U.S. 483, https://supreme.justia.com/cases/federal/us/533/483 [journalist did not grant electronic republication rights for collective work]; (d) *Eldred v. Ashcroft*, 537 U.S. 186, https://supreme.justia.com/cases/federal/us/537/186 [duration of copyright]; (e) *Metro-Goldwyn-Mayer v. Grokster*, 545 U.S. 913, https://supreme.justia.com/cases/federal/us/545/913 [copyright infringement]; (f) *Reed Elsevier v. Muchnick*, 559 U.S. 154, https://supreme.justia.com/cases/federal/us/559/154 [copyright infringement case]; (g) *Golan v. Holder*, 565 U.S. 302, https://supreme.justia.com/cases/federal/us/565/302 [copyright in public domain case]; and (h) *Kirtsaeng v. John Wiley & Sons, Inc.*, 568 U.S. 519, https://supreme.justia.com/cases/federal/us/568/519 [this is the most important copyright cases since the *Bobbs-Merrill v. Strauss* 210 U.S. 339 case in 1908; the Court voted that the first sale doctrine applies to copyrighted works made lawfully overseas]. Also see Albert N. Greco. "The Kirtsaeng and SCI-HUB Cases: The Major U.S. Copyright Cases in the Twenty-First Century," *Publishing Research Quarterly 33*, 3(September 2017): 238–253.
26. Albert N. Greco. The Scholarly Publishing Community Should Support Changes to U.S. Copyright Law," *Journal of Scholarly Publishing 49*, 2(January 2018): 248–259.
27. Greco. "Book Publishers Should Support Changes in the Office of the Copyright and the Register of Copyrights," *Publishing Research Quarterly 33*, 2(June 2017): 117–125.

28. United States District Court, Southern District of New York. "Elsevier Inc., Elsevier B.V., and Elsevier LTD. Against www.sci-hub.com, The Library Genesis Project, dba LIBGEN.org, Alexandra Elbakyan, and John Does 1–77;" https://cases.justia.com/federal/district-courts/newyork/nysdce/1:2015cv04282/442951/53/0.pdf.
29. Ibid.
30. Ibid.
31. Some of the pirate book websites include: www.4shared.com; www.uploaded.net; www.booksos.com; www.book4you.com; www.rapidgator.net; and www.bookzz.org. The site Z-library was closed by the F.B.I.
32. Anna's Archive; https://annas-archive.org.

CHAPTER 6

The Future of the Humanities and Scholarly Publishing in the Humanities

Abstract For thousands of years, the humanities were at the center of higher education. Unfortunately, in the twentieth century, and extending into the twenty-first-century, the humanities confronted a series of major crises that undermined the preeminence of the humanities in higher education. This chapter presents a series of suggestions and strategies, some employing the theories of Ted Levitt's "Marketing Myopia" article, which could assist the humanities in addressing some of the debilitating crises, including working with universities, the National Endowment for the Humanities, and the National Endowment for the Arts.

Keywords Humanities • Crisis in the humanities • Open access • cOAlition S • Plan S • Open access mandates • Economics of scholarly publishing • Academic libraries • University presses • Commercial scholarly publishers • Humanities strategies • Humanities council • Future of the humanities

A. N. Greco, *Scholarly Publishing in the Humanities, 2000–2024*, Marketing and Communication in Higher Education, https://doi.org/10.1007/978-3-031-66170-9_6

INTRODUCTION

Certain substantive issues need to be addressed in order to understand the future of the humanities and scholarly publishing in the humanities in the United States. First, the humanities are not a monolithic entity. In reality, faculty members are in an academic department (perhaps history) and/or at some colleges in a program (perhaps American Studies comprised of faculty members in English language and literature, history, fine arts, etc.). So, the vast majority of faculty members view primarily their academic discipline rather than the humanities as a complete entity. There is a need to broaden this view to incorporate the wants and needs of faculty members in different humanities fields.

Second, according to data from the U.S. Department of Education (Education), National Center for Education Statistics (NCES) there were 3646 non-profit colleges in the United States in 2021 employing 1.79 million faculty members.[1] However, 110 colleges, mainly small, liberal arts colleges, closed their doors since 2016, triggering the termination of humanities and other faculty members. These closings have contributed to yet another crisis in the humanities. Table 6.1 has the data.

Clearly, there are a myriad of possible "ideas" or "solutions" regarding how humanities faculty members, as well as academic administrators, can address and seek to possibly minimize, or hopefully eliminate some of the crises in the humanities. However, there is no "one size fits all" strategy that makes sense for a community college in Paramus, N.J., a liberal arts college in Grinnell, Iowa, or a major university in Palo Alto, C.A.

UNDERSTANDING THE ECONOMICS OF SCHOLARLY PUBLISHING IN THE HUMANITIES

However, it is exceptionally important for faculty members in the humanities to understand the basic "economics of scholarly publishing," including the emergence and growth of mandatory open access (OA) policies and procedures, the decline in the sales of printed scholarly monographs, and digital publishing options. After all, academics have to interact with a myriad of individuals at scholarly journals and scholarly books, which include university presses, societies, and commercial scholarly publishers.

In the past few years, the OA movement picked up traction in Europe regarding the prices of scholarly journals in the science, technology, and medical (STM) category. "The open access movement argues that

Table 6.1 Number of U.S. college closings since 2016 by state

State	Number of closed colleges
Alabama	2
California	8
Colorado	1
Connecticut	2
Delaware	1
Florida	2
Iowa	1
Illinois	9
Indiana	5
Kansas	1
Kentucky	1
Massachusetts	10
Maryland	1
Maine	1
Michigan	4
Minnesota	1
Missouri	4
North Carolina	1
Nebraska	2
New Hampshire	2
New Jersey	1
Nevada	1
New York	11
Ohio	6
Oklahoma	1
Oregon	5
Pennsylvania	6
South Dakota	2
Tennessee	5
Texas	1
Virginia	1
Vermont	6
Washington	1
Wisconsin	2
West Virginia	2
Total number of college closings	110

Source: Inside Higher Education; https://www.highereddive.com/news/how-many-colleges-and-universities-have-closed-since-2016/539379

scientific research funded by public money should not be protected behind expensive subscription [pay walls] but should be available free of charge to public scrutiny."[2]

cOAlition S has detailed information about the goal to achieve full and immediate free OA access to scholarly STM publications. "Plan S is an initiative for Open Access publishing that was launched in September 2018... Plan S requires that, from 2021, scientific publications that result from research funded by public grants must be published in compliant Open Access journals or platforms."[3] Their website has more detailed information about the development and creation of OA mandates and its supporters.

> On 4 September 2018, a group of national research funding organizations, with the support of the European Commission and the European Research Council (ERC), announced the launch of cOAlition S... It [cOAlition S] is built around Plan S, which consists of one target and 10 principles. cOAlition S signals the commitment to implement the necessary measures to fulfil its main principle. 'With effect from 2021, all scholarly publications on the results from research funded by public or private grants provided by national, regional and international research councils and funding bodies, must be published in Open Access Journals, on Open Access Platforms, or made immediately available through Open Access Repositories without embargo.' The initiative was born from the cooperation between the heads of the participating Research Funding Organizations, Marc Schiltz the President of Science Europe, and Robert-Jan Smits, previously the Open Access Envoy of the European Commission. It also drew on significant input from the Scientific Council of the ERC. cOAlition S funders (a group of national research funders, European and international organizations and charitable foundations) have agreed to implement the 10 principles of Plan S in a coordinated way, together with the European Commission and the ERC. Other research funders from across the world, both public and private, are invited to join cOAlition.[4]

Plan S addressed scientific journal publishing issues in Europe, although it was hoped that OA would be adopted in other regions. How do the humanities fit into the movement toward OA? The philosophy behind the development of the OA STM movement was contained in an article about the alleged academic "oligopoly" in scholarly publishing written by Vincent Lariviere, Stephenie Haustein, and Philippe Mongeon. This article captured the attention of a large number of academics in Europe and then the rest of the world, including the United States. These three authors wrote that a small cluster of academic journal STM publishers controlled more than 50% of all scholarly scientific papers published in 2013. This alleged concentration, when combined with what the authors insisted were high annual subscription prices of scholarly journals with high citation indices and in the "must have" STM journals, created what they insisted was an "oligopoly of academic publishing in the digital era."[5] The answer to this "oligopoly" was the creation of a system whereby all scholarly research, often supported by European state-supported institutions or by European governmental or other research funds, should be free. In essence, they called for the end of the established subscription-based system of publishing. Ironically, the OA advocates never addressed who would pay for the "free" journals.

It was only a matter of time before the concept of OA in the scientific, technical, and medical sector migrated into the social sciences and eventually into the humanities. Margot Finn wrote a major 2019 report for the Royal Historical Society entitled "Plan S and the History Journal Landscape." Finn remarked that "this report from the Royal Historical Society (RHS) assesses the extent of history journals' engagement with, and preparation for, implementation of Plan S-aligned open access (OA) mandates... This report provided evidence, information, and guidance for history researchers, editors of journals, learned societies, publishers, research organizations, and grant-making bodies in the context of ULRI's [the grant making body] forthcoming public consultation on OA."[6]

Eventually, OA impacted scholars in the humanities interested in publishing scholarly journal articles. *Nature*, a preeminent scholarly journal, outlined the options academics had in the new OA publishing environment. "Traditional subscription publishing model: an article is submitted and is assessed by our editors. If suitable, it will be put through peer review, and, if successful will be eligible for publication....Published articles are made available to institutions and individuals who subscribe to *Nature* or who pay to read specific articles."[7] *Nature* also outlined the "gold open access" model. "The author/s or funders pay an Article Processing Charge (APC). The final version of the published article is then free to read for everyone."[8]

Obviously, the OA guidelines pertained originally to STM academics with research grants. Very few scholars in the humanities receive research grants with funds that could be used to pay an APC. However, OA journal articles, or OA books, had to comply with the evolving Plan S guidelines that morphed eventually into mandates. The basic economic issue that confronted university presses, societies, and commercial academic publishers centered on the need to charge APCs or book processing charges since, first, someone has to pay the costs associated with publishing printed or digital articles and books, and second, the never-ending expenses to create, upgrade, and protect a computer database of the articles or books from hackers and pirates and the never-ending legal costs to litigate when copyright infringement and/or piracy occurred.

The Economics of Scholarly Publishing

So what were the costs to publish an OA scholarly journal or book? APCs vary significantly in the journal sector. For example, the APC for *Publishing Research Quarterly*, which publishes articles about various aspects of book or journal publishing, was (in 2024) $3090.00.[9] In the STM sector, APCs can exceed $10,000.00. While these are expensive journal APCs, the OA costs paid for by a faculty member for a scholarly monograph published by a university press or a commercial scholarly publisher was significantly higher, often between $10,000 and $20,000.

An excellent detailed analysis of monographic costs was prepared by Nancy Maron, Charlotte Mulhern, Daniel Rossman, and Kimberly Schmelzinger. Their analyses in 2016 created four categories of U.S. university presses: group 1 had annual revenues under $1.5 million; group 2: between $1.5 million and $3.0 million; group 3: between $3.0 million and $6.0 million; and group 4: revenues beyond $6.0 million.

Their results for the average group costs to publish a monograph, and the average number of new books published in each category were as follows: group 1: $30,091 per new title, and the average number of new title: 48.6; group 2: $44,906 and 76.0 books; group 3: $34,098 and 123.2 books; and group 4: $49,155 and 252.6 books.[10]

The authors utilized various costs to ascertain the average cost of these books (N.B.: not all of the books in their study were in the humanities), including staff costs, title-specific direct costs, press as well as level overhead, and in-kind. For example, for group 1: staff costs: $14,796; staff overhead: $3310; direct costs: $4460; press-level overhead: $9958; in-kind: $2370; basic: $22,550; full cost: $30,091; and full-cost plus: $34,887.[11]

Drilling down into group 1's costs, the authors indicated the following: average staff costs per monograph, by activities: acquisitions: $8159; manuscript editorial: $2326; production: $843; design: $1532; marketing: $1938; and total staff expenses: $14,798.[12]

Fortunately, the authors addressed costs for group 2 to publish books in the humanities, which included (a) African-American studies: number of pages 200; illustrations: 19; staff time costs: $34,246; number of people who worked on the book: 14; basic cost: $50,578; full cost: $66,506; (b) history: number of pages 480; illustrations: 53; staff time costs: $32,348; number of people who worked on the book: 10; basic cost: $52,881; and full cost: $74,536; and (c) biography: number of pages 536; illustrations: 51; staff time costs: $33,238; number of people who worked on the book: 15; basic cost: $62,534; and full cost: $80,534.[13]

Open Access Monographic Costs

The movement toward open access monographs was addressed by Laura Brown, Maya Dayan, Brenna McLoughlin, Roger C. Schoenfeld, John Sherer, and Erich van Rijn in a well received and publicized 2023 Ithaka report "Print Revenue and Open Access Monographs." The authors concluded that OA titles, with both hard cover and paperback formats, can generate significant print and digital revenues. However, sales vary significantly by academic field. Title revenues in the STM sector generated average revenues of $88,349 (probably because of research funds to support an OA book's processing charges); and computer science topped the list at $292,709 (again probably because researchers in this academic field have research funds to support OA). Unfortunately the revenues for humanities titles were rather low, including arts and humanities: $7980 and history: $6523.[14] So the Ithaka report's support for the viability of OA must be viewed as being accurate regarding the research-funded STM sectors but more cautious regarding the humanities.

Humanities Books, Libraries, and University Presses

Books in the humanities have been published for centuries in Europe (since 1478 at Oxford) and since the late nineteenth century in the United States by university presses and commercial scholarly publishers. However, in what could be described as "unsettling times," with high inflations and sharp increase in the costs associated with publishing and marketing printed books, can university presses, even those at major American universities, continue to publish books in the humanities? Are university presses impacted by the basic laws of supply and demand? Will university presses be compelled to curtail the output of humanities books?

Scott Jaschik reported in 2015 in *Inside Higher Education* that there was a sharp increase in the publication of books in the humanities. "The increase in the number of humanities books published is important to humanities professors not only for the scholarship produced and shared, but for its impact on careers…The monograph remains the 'gold standard' for evaluating humanities scholarship."[15] Carl Straumsheim, also in *Inside Higher Education*, indicated that in 2017 "the market for original humanities monographs may be shrinking, according to a report on the output of [American] university presses… If the market is in decline, it could be a sign that the university presses that publish those monographs are struggling—and indeed many presses have closed or scaled back their operations."[16]

The market for humanities books has been traditionally academics, students, general readers, and libraries; traditionally libraries accounted for a large percent of all sales. Rick Anderson, writing for *The Scholarly Kitchen*, wondered how important are library sales to university presses? Analyzing 326 scholarly books published by the University of Chicago Press, Anderson reported that 51.35% of Chicago's 40 history titles in the study were sold to libraries in this nation and abroad. Other humanities titles also exhibited large library sales, including art and art history: 41.87%, literary studies: 52.74%, music: 58.81%, philosophy 43.35%, and religious studies 39.86%.[17] Elizabeth A. Jones and Paul N. Courant, in the *Journal of Scholarly Publishing*, wrote that "in scholarly publishing circles, the story of how university presses have been crushed under the weight of declining library monograph budgets has achieved the status of a canonical truth… Put simply, we care about the health of university presses because we care about how knowledge is produced and distributed."[18]

Jeremiads about the state of university presses sparked a number of articles defending the role and importance of these presses in the intellectual fabric of the nation and indeed the world. For example, Margaret Renld, in *The New York Times*, posited that university presses were keeping American literature alive.[19] Peter Berkery and Annette Windhorn, executives at the Association of University Presses (AUP), wrote about the ethical imperative of the university press.[20] The executive council of the Modern Language Association (MLA) wrote that "the MLA regards university presses as vital to the dissemination of scholarship on languages and literatures and to the scholarly accreditation process, which is indispensable to the academic community. The defunding of university presses puts an inordinate strain on humanities scholars who depend on presses at all stages of their careers for publication and circulation of their work for their professional livelihood."[21]

Stanford University is one the nation's preeminent institutions of higher education. The university also has a well-respected university press. As of August 31, 2023, this university's endowment stood at $36.5 billion. This endowment "provided an enduring source of financial support for fulfillment of the university's mission of teaching, learning, and research. It disbursed a $1.7 billion payout to support vital academic programs."[22] However, four years earlier in 2019, the university announced that it planned to cut the university's annual subsidy to its university press. "Stanford has the world's third-largest university endowment, valued in 2018 at $26.5 billion. Yet it is crying poverty to explain why it can no longer provide yearly $1.7 million subsidies to its acclaimed [university] press... Stanford's press, with a staff of 35, makes about $5 million in [annual] revenue from the 130 to 135 books it releases each year in 14 disciplines... Book publishing by university presses is not usually profitable and is not meant to be, said [Gregory M.] Brittan [the editorial director at Johns Hopkins University Press]."[23] Stanford's decision to cut the annual subsidy triggered a number of responses, including public support for Stanford's press from the Association of University Presses[24] and the Stanford University Senate.[25] Ilya Somin, in *The Atlantic,* asked several pivotal questions. "What is the purpose of a university press? Should it be expected to support itself"? Somin's conclusion was that university presses should not have to make a profit and need university financial support in order to survive.[26] With this level of national negative publicity, the university decided to extend the press subsidy for another year (i.e., 2020).[27]

It was clear, in reviewing the Stanford situation, that a major university press could not cover its expenses only with the sales of scholarly monographs and related income. Unfortunately, the reality of scholarly monographic book revenue short-falls has impacted the majority of university presses. Carl Straumshein interviewed Charles T. Watkinson, the director of the University of Michigan Press. Michigan is a major university press in the United States. Watkinson remarked that sales at his press "have reached a point where the press now needs the decline to level off. It is clear that this is not a sustainable situation... In fiscal year 2005, the press published 155 titles, selling 292,407 copies and generating more than $5 million in sales revenues. Eleven years later [2016], the press is publishing and selling less... unit sales 143,319. Sales revenue has plummeted about 40%... Watkinson pointed to the collapse of the market for print monographs."[28]

The traditional printed monograph has remained at the center of scholarship in the humanities for decades.[29] However, there are a number of serious questions that must be addressed by humanities faculty members, department chairs, deans, and provosts about printed books. If the sale of printed monographs are in a state of decline, what is the future?[30] If the monograph in any format is important, who will pay for the publication of monographs?[31] Is the current university press organizational structure efficient and able to respond to substantive challenges? Will the humanities be compelled to confront the death of the printed monograph and transition to e-books and/or writing a series of scholarly articles or book reviews in order to gain tenure and promotion?[32] Who will print scholarly monographs? This is a concern of university press directors and their production staff members. According to data in the *Statistical Abstract of the United States 2024,* between 2000 and 2022 (the last year of available data) there has been an unsettling 47.38% decline in the number of commercial printing establishments (many of which print books) in the United States dropping from 39,035 in 2000 to only 20,542 in 2022. Of that total, approximately 100 U.S. printing companies print books.[33]

Pew Research's 2022 report on book reading in the United States provides a possible answer to many of these questions. Pew reported that three-in-ten Americans read e-books. Looking closely at Pew's statistics revealed the following: college graduates, 39% read e-books and 32% listened to audiobooks; Americans 18–29, 42% read e-books and 30% listened to audiobooks; Americans 30–49, 32% e-books usage and 27% audiobooks.[34] In order to publish scholarly monographs, hard-pressed university presses, that often sell fewer than 500 copies of a printed monographic book (and too frequently sell fewer than 300 copies), should consider (a) adopting a print-on-demand (POD) system; (b) printing a very small number of hardcover or paperback monographs, maybe 30 to 50 copies for the author and internal use by editors and publishers; and (c) utilizing ultimately and probably exclusively the digital e-book option, and possibly audiobooks and podcasts, for the majority of sales. In essence, scholarly book publishers might have to consider adopting the marketing strategies of the big trade book publishing firms (e.g., Penguin Random House Macmillan) and the college textbook publishers (e.g., Pearson, Cengage) to launch and maintain a strategy based on emphasizing a commitment to understanding and coping with changing market conditions. This means utilizing the basic marketing theories of Ted Levitt in his important article "Marketing Myopia."

Levitt's article emphasized a number of salient points, including (a) "many companies declined inevitably as technology advanced because they defined themselves too narrowly; (b) to continue growing, companies must determine and act on their customer's wants and needs and desires and not assume on the longevity of their product(s); and (c) there are four key components in an effective marketing strategy: development, production, distribution, and promotion... The railroads ended up in trouble not because the need for passengers and freight transportation declined. They declined because this need was not filled by railroads. Railroads were really in the transportation business...They were product oriented and not market oriented. "[35] Levitt famously said that "people don't want a quarter-inch drill. They want quarter-inch holes."[36]

University presses and commercial scholarly publishers disseminate information. Since Gutenberg, this information was printed in a book. The Pew Research finding emphasized the growing e-book usage in the United States among college graduates (including faculty members in the humanities) and Americans between 18–29 and 30–49 (college and graduate school students and humanities faculty members in the 30–49 age cohort). The movement toward e-book adoption and possibly e-book exclusivity in the scholarly publishing sector, assuming a continuation of the peer review process, is a viable strategy that can address the pressing financial situation of declining printed monographic sales, especially at university presses that lack endowments. A review of digital e-book options in the commercial scholarly publishing universe confirms that many of the largest commercial firms have adopted the digital option, and book processing fees were in the +$15,000 range.

What if open access or e-books became popular or the norm in the humanities? Kindsay McKenzie reported in 2018 that two of the nation's important university presses, MIT and Michigan, "announced plans to start selling their e-book collections directly to libraries by creating their own distribution platforms...to move away from these third party platforms, known as aggregators."[37] Watkinson at Michigan outlined who would pay for their e-book collection. "The list price for the University of Michigan e-book collection would be $6,800, but university libraries will pay between $694 and $5,760 per year based on their size...to approximately 1,000 titles in the publisher's back catalog."[38] In May 2024, MIT press announced its new direct-to-open access program (D2O). The MIT's press release indicated that "D2O is a sustainable framework for open access monographs that shifts publishing from a solely market-based purchase model where individuals and libraries buy single e-books to a collaborative, library-supported open access model."[39] Both MIT and Michigan stressed that OA articles and OA books receive higher use and citations than the traditional subscription-based journals or monographs sold into the traditional channels of distribution. The citation advantage of OA journals was analyzed by Allison Langham-Putrow, Caitlin Bakker, and Amy Riegelman in an important PLOS ONE article in 2021.[40]

So, new theories about who will pay for the open access journals and books emerged in recent years. Libraries could make annual purchases of a complete collection of e-books, whether they need any or all of the 80+ new annual titles. cOAlition S suggested that the research community could establish "a community based scholarly communication system...that enables research funders, in collaboration with other key stakeholders."[41] Another option would be for libraries to adopt the policies of the "Dutch UKB coalition of research libraries [that] signed up to the very first of what are now known as transformative agreements (TAs)...TAs which bundle the cost of open access (OA) publishing with subscription deals."[42]

Can the good intentions of community support organizations, academic libraries, faculty members, departments (or programs) in the humanities, university presses, universities, and funders support the OA movement in the humanities? The answer is, at best, a qualified "maybe." If academics in the humanities have learned anything from their colleagues in economics and finance, they know there is no "free lunch." And the costs associated with OA journals are high, and the Open access (OA)OA expenditures for books are very expensive. If Stanford had second thoughts about a $1.7 million allocation to its university press, how many universities and their libraries have the financial resources to participate in community funding processes? These issues were addressed by Christina Lembrecht in an article in *The Times Higher Education*. Lembrecht wrote that "if authors must pay, most humanities scholarship will never be open access."[43] Loren B. Byrne, in *Nature*, maintained that open access publishing fees "particularly disadvantages researchers in low-and middle-income countries. APCs can also pose a challenge for some scholars in high-income countries. This often-overlooked group includes academics who, like me, are based at small, less-resources institutions... [We] must publish peer-reviewed articles to receive tenure, promotion, and merit-based awards... The APCs for one open access article can exceed the entire annual institutional allocation [at Byrne's college] for professional development."[44]

"Who Was Paid?'

However, the initial debate over "who will pay" OA journal and book processing charges shifted to another question. "Who was paid?"

A series of new highly cited "oligopoly" articles were published; the original "oligopoly" view was centered originally on the subscription prices of STM scholarly journals by commercial academic publishers. The new emphasis shifted to the APCs charged by these same commercial scholarly publishers. The 2023 research of Leigh-Ann Butler, Lisa Matthias, Marc-Andre Simard, Philippe Mongeon, and Stafanie Haustein indicated that "using publication data from WoS, OA status from Unpaywall, and national APC prices from open databases and historical fees retrieved via the Internet Archive Wayback Machine, we estimate that globally authors paid $1.06 billion in [article processing] publication fees to these publishers from 2015–2018."[45] Fei Shu and Vincent Lariviere's research, also in 2023, indicated that "the adoption of OA publishing may not necessarily lead to a decrease in the overall cost of knowledge dissemination, as Article Processing Charges (APCs) can create an additional financial burden for scholars."[46]

However, the editors and publishers at the commercial scholarly publishing firms and university presses have a fiduciary responsibility to the owners of the company or the board of directors at a university. So, at the end of the day, OA digital publishing has expenses that must be covered in order to avoid a fiscal problem for the firm or the university, thus the creation of processing charges.

Other Possible Strategies for the Humanities

If the humanities faced a series of crises that at times seemed overwhelming and almost insurmountable, the humanities could consider adopting some rather aggressive marketing strategies built on the basic tenets of Ted Levitt. Some possible strategies include the following.

First, create an inclusive college-wide humanities council. This council can target current and possible future student and academic administrator audiences, and the council can stress the benefits and opportunities of a degree in the humanities to students and to administrators. The council can sponsor a series of events during the academic year. For example, a humanities day in the fall and spring semesters addressing jobs for under-graduate humanities students.[47] Another option would be the creation of a student humanities research day, with undergraduates and/or graduate students presenting their research. Many college libraries offer students and faculty members the opportunity to launch (and the library would maintain) a student research journal. The library often creates a "research commons" and the journal is hosted on the library website through an arrangement with bepress' "Digital Commons" operation.[48]

In addition, the humanities council could highlight important events in the history of the humanities. One example would be a series of lectures addressing the humanities research of the female winners of the Nobel Prize in Literature. "Seventeen women have been awarded the Nobel Prize in Literature. Swedish author Selma Lagerlöf (1858–1940) was the first woman to be awarded in 1909. Selma Lagerlöf was awarded five years before she was elected to the Swedish Academy, the Nobel Prize awarding institution responsible for selecting Nobel Prize laureates in literature."[49] The 17 women awarded the Nobel Prize in Literature are as follows: in 1909, Selma Lagerlöf; 1926, Grazia Deledda; 1928, Sigrid Undset; 1938, Pearl Buck; 1945, Gabriela Mistral; 1966, Nelly Sachs; 1991, Nadine Gordimer; 1993, Toni Morrison; 1996, Wislawa Szymborska; 2004, Elfriede Jelinek; 2007, Doris Lessing; 2009, Herta Müller; 2013, Alice Munro; 2015, Svetlana Alexievich; 2018, Olga Tokarczuk; 2020, Louise Glück; and 2022, Annie Ernaux.

Yet another lecture series could address certain authors as well as the creation of important book publishing companies that published substan-tive fiction and non-fiction books in the humanities (e.g., 2024 will be the 100th anniversary of the birth of James Baldwin; in 2027 Random House will be 100 years old; and Toni Morrison was a book editor at Random House. Another major event in 2025 will be the 100th anniversary of the publication of *The Great Gatsby* and the 50th anniversary of the release of the Robert Redford-Mia Farrow *The Great Gatsby* movie).

The humanities council could make documents available from *Fortune* business magazine (and other publications) that provide realistic informa-tion about employment after graduation for students who major in the humanities, including: "The Rise of the English Major: BlackRock COO Wants To recruit Liberal Arts Analysts That Have Nothing to Do With

Finance or Technology";[50] "IBM AI Chief Advises People Who Want A Tech Job in 2024 to Learn the Language and Creative Thinking Skills You get With the Liberal Arts";[51] and "Why Critics Are Wrong About Liberal Arts Degrees."[52] In addition, there are informative studies from the U.S. Department of Labor (Labor), Bureau of Labor Statistics (BLS) that address important issues for undergraduates, including "What Can I Do with My Liberal Arts Degree?"[53]

Second, the college humanities council could reach out to local, county, state, or the federal government humanities councils and work with them and participate in their numerous activities. The National Endowment for the Humanities (NEH) "supports local humanities programs and events. The council are funded in part by the federal government through NEH's Office of Federal State Partnership."[54] Every state has a state and jurisdictional humanities council. "Working with local, state, or federal museums offers faculty and students the opportunity to gain useful research training. The Institute of Museum and Library Services advances "supports and empowers American museums, libraries, and related organizations through grantmaking, research, and policy development."[55]

Third, the college humanities council should address the impact of open access (OA) fees on scholarly publishing in the humanities. Very few humanities scholars have access to research grants from a funding organization within or outside the college, So, the widespread adoption of mandatory OA requirements in the humanities in the United States could be the major crisis threatening the scholarly output of academics.

However, the humanities have adopted various digital options including "digital humanities," a movement that the humanities council should stress. David M. Berry, at the British Academy, insisted that "digital humanities" "are at the leading edge of applying computer-based technology in the humanities... The field has grown tremendously... It originally focused on developing digital tools and the creation of archives and databases for texts, artworks, and other materials... Digital humanities incorporate key insights from languages and literature, history, music, media and communications, computer science and information studies and combine these different approaches into new frameworks."[56]

Fourth, the humanities council could hold a series of seminars, and seek funding to support these seminars and research, outlining the importance of the "digital humanities" for research and employment. For example, the humanities council could contact the NEH's Office of Digital Humanities (ODH). "ODH offers grant programs that fund project teams experimenting with digital technologies to develop new methodologies for humanities research, teaching and learning, public engagement, and scholarly communications. ODH funds those studying digital technology from a humanistic perspective and humanists seeking to create digital publications."[57]

NEH also offers the Digital Humanities Advancement Grants program (DHAG), and the humanities council could consider contacting this office. DHAG "supports innovative, experimental, and/or computationally challenging digital projects, leading to work that can scale to enhance scholarly research, teaching, and public programming in the humanities. The DHAG program supports projects... that contribute to and supports the humanities, such as open-source code, tools, or platforms; evaluative studies that investigate the practices and the impact of digital scholarship on research, pedagogy, scholarly communication, and public engagement."[58]

Fifth, the National Endowment for the Arts (NEA) sponsors the "Big Read" program. "The National Endowment for the Arts Big Read... broadens our understanding of ourselves and our neighbors through the power of a shared reading experience. The goals of the NEA Big Read are to inspire meaningful conversations, celebrate local creativity, elevate a wide variety of voices and perspectives, and build stronger connections in each community."[59] Financial support is available from the NEA. "The National Endowment for the Arts (NEA)... is pleased to announce grants to 62 nonprofit organizations for NEA Big Read programming in 2024–2025. In total, the NEA is investing $1,075,000 to support programming centered around a book from the NEA Big Read Library, with the goal of inspiring meaningful conversations, celebrating local creativity, elevating a wide variety of voices and perspectives, and building stronger connections in each community. Community programming during this cycle is focused on the theme 'Where We Live.' Grantees chose their NEA Big Read book based on how its themes, characters, and setting relate to the unique aspects of their community. They will use this selection as inspiration for book discussions, writing workshops, and creative activities in collaboration with a range of local partners...With every page turned, the NEA Big Read fosters understanding, empathy, and connection," said Maria Rosario Jackson, PhD, chair of the National Endowment for the Arts. "Through a shared reading experience, our NEA Big Read grantees will explore their collective story and sense of place, cultivating a deeper appreciation for the diverse narratives that make up our beautiful and complex communities."[60]

Sixth, in support of its efforts to advance national information infrastructures in libraries and archives, and subject to the availability of funds and agency discretion,

> the Institute of Museum and Library Services (IMLS) anticipates providing funding through this program. These funds may support DHAG projects that further the IMLS mission to advance, support, and empower America's libraries, archives, museums, and related organizations. IMLS funding supports innovative collaborations between library and archives professionals, humanities professionals, information scientists, and relevant public communities that advance the preservation of, access to, and public engagement with, digital collections and services. IMLS encourages DHAG applicants to work in collaboration, and employ the expertise of, library and archives staff at your institution or across the country to strengthen knowledge networks, empower community learning, foster civic cohesion, advance research, and support the traditionally underserved.[61]

Seventh, the humanities council could lobby to obtain additional, or new, research funds from the university and/or governmental and/or corporate and independent funding organizations. Traditionally, at least in the years before World War II, American research funds originated primarily within the university. The war sparked an intense push to obtain government funds to conduct scientific research, and this pattern of government-supported research, and complemented by corporate research funds, continued in the nation after the war. Richard Drake, writing in the *American Scholar*, remarked that "the intellectual integrity of university research, however, is today [September 2019] beset with difficulties caused by corporate and government pressures on the schools. To survive, research universities need the money that only corporations and government can bestow in sufficient amounts. Such patrons as these are not in business for artistic and intellectual aims alone."[62] Audrey Williams June, in a 2014 article in *The Chronicle of Higher Education*, reported that American "colleges spent $97.8 billion on research and development in the 2022 fiscal year, up $8 billion from the year before, according to new data from the National Sciences Foundation."[63] These funds addressed funded research in a number of fields, including materials science ($286 million), engineering fields "not elsewhere classified" ($2.467 billion), metallurgical and materials engineering ($887 million), social science fields "not elsewhere classified" ($1.26 billion), life sciences fields "not elsewhere classified" ($1.518 billion), chemistry ($2127 billion), and health sciences ($31.87 billion).[64] The three universities that received the largest research funds in 2022 included Johns Hopkins ($3.4 billion), the University of California, San Francisco ($1.806 billion), and the University of Pennsylvania ($1.791 billion).[65] The humanities have been underfunded for decades, and attempts could be initiated to address what is a serious funding problem for the humanities.

CONCLUSION

For several thousand years, the humanities were at the center of education, and specifically higher education. Clearly, the humanities have faced a series of debilitating crises that, in many ways, undermined the traditional role the humanities played in the education of citizens. Some of the crises were, and remain today, beyond the control of humanities faculties, departments, and programs including the perception of the importance of STM research and funding and the rising costs of a college education.[66]

However, a number of the crises and troubling events could be addressed specifically and thoughtfully by humanists. The creation of a humanities council could spark discussions within the university, in undergraduate and graduate seminars, and in the research studies about substantive issues of concern to the humanities and the entire university, including the apparent misalignment of incentives (i.e., tenure and promotion) within many colleges,[67] the role of artificial intelligence (AI) in instruction and research,[68] the need for more financial support for university presses and academic libraries,[69] the belief that scholarly publishing today is a cultural and economic concern and not just a technological issue,[70] and finally the belief that the majority of issues that have created crises in the humanities are not permanent.[71]

There are a number of important scholarly books about the humanities that could be used in humanities seminars and in out-reach programs. For example, Helen Small, in *The Value of the Humanities*,[72] and *The Liberating Arts: Why We Need Liberal Arts Education* edited by Jeffrey Bilbro, Jessica Hooten Wilson, and David Henreckson[73] provide coherent analyses why the humanities have been, and remain, of critical importance to society and students.

This belief was discussed by Martha C. Nussbaum in an NEH interview. Nussbaum maintained that "we are lucky in the United States to have our liberal arts system...There are three points you can make. The one I think should be front and center is that the humanities prepare students to be good citizens…Secondly, we need to emphasize their economic value. Business Leaders love the humanities because they know that to innovate you need more than rote knowledge… The third point is about the search for meaning."[74]

Nussbaum was correct. The humanities have played the substantive role in the development of education for thousands of years. While the humanities confront serious challenges, they will remain at the heart of higher education for the coming decades as long as academics in the humanities understand clearly and address the current and future challenges confronting the humanities.

However, as Ted Levitt maintained, scholars in the diverse humanities cannot rely exclusively on past arguments and the prevalent future of the humanities circa 2000. After all, the thoughts of the "poet laureate" of the Bronx, N.Y. ring true even today. "The future isn't what it used to be."[75]

Notes

1. U.S. Department of Education (Education). National Center for Education Statistics (NCES. "Fast Facts: Educational Institutions;" https://www.nces.ed.gov/programs/digect/d22_105.50.asp.
2. Christopher Balme. "Editorial: Open Access Revised Plan S;" https://doi.org/10.1353/fmt.2019.0000. Also see Sponsoring Consortium for Open Access Publishing in Particle Physics. "SCOAP³;" https://scoap3.org/what-is-scoap3.
3. cOAlition S. "Plan S: Making Full and Immediate Open Access a Reality;" https://www.coalition-s.org. Also see Laval Liverpool. "Open Access Reformers Launch Next Bold Publishing Plan;" https://www.nature.com/articles/d41586-023-03342-6.
4. Ibid. Also see Lisa Janicke Hinchcliffe, Rick Anderson, Hasseb Irfanullah, Roy Kaufman, and Angela Cochran. "Ask the Chefs: cOAlitionS's 'Towards Responsible Publishing';" https://scholarlykitchen.sspnet.org/2023/11/16/ask-the-chefs-coalition-ss-towards-responsible-publishing. Curtis Brundy, Laura Hanscom, Barbara Kern, and Bridgette Weinsteiger. "Guest Post: Open Access to University Press Frontlists: A Call to Action;" https://scholarlykitchen.sspnet.org/2023/09/20/guest-post-open-access-to-university-press-frontlists-a-call-to-action.
5. Vincent Lariviere, Stephenie Haustein, and Philippe Mongeon. "The Oligopoly of Academic Publishing in the Digital Era," https://www.doi.org/10.1371journal.pone.0127502. Also see *The Financial Times*. "How

Academic Publishers Profit From the Publish or Perish Culture;" https://www.ft.com/content/575f72a8-4eb2-4538-87a8-7652d67d499e. Many scholars who insisted that an "oligopoly" charging subscription fees had to be replaced by OA fees, paid by STM research grants, which would enable scholarship to be read for free later has second thoughts when APCs were implemented. See James Friedman. "Chapter 11: Oligopoly Theory," *Handbook of Mathematical Economics* 2(1982): 491–534 Friedman wrote that "the oligopoly theory usually refers to the partial equilibrium study of markets in which the demand side is competitive, while the supply side is neither monopolized nor competitive."

6. Margot Finn. "Plan S and the History Journal Landscape;" https://files.royalhistsoc.org/wp-content/uploads/2019/10/17204855/RHS_PlanS_Full_Report__Oct19_FINAL-WEB.pdf. Also see Rick Anderson. "Why Are There Virtually No Mandatory Open Access Policies at American Universities?" https://onlinelibrary.wiley.com/doi/full/10.1002/leap.1034. Anthony J. Olejinczak and Molly J. Wilson. "Who's Writing Open Access (OA) Articles? Characteristics of OA Authors at Ph.D. Granting Institutions in the United States;" https://direct.mit.edu/qss/article/1/4/1429/96127/Who-s-writing-open-access-OA-articles.

7. Nature. "Publishing Options;" https://www.nature.com/nature/for-authors/publiahing-options. Also see SPARC (Scheme for Promoting Academic and Research Collaborations). "Open Access;" https://sparcopen.org/open-access. SPARC. "U.S. Taxpayers Are Entitled to Access the Results of the Research They Fund;" https://sparcopen.org/wp-content/uploads/2021/11/SPARC-oa-policy-one-pager.pdf.

8. Ibid. Also see Springer Nature. "The Fundamentals of Open Access and Open Research;" https://www.springernature.com/gp/open-research/about/the-fundamentals-of-open-access-and-open-research. Also see Anat Hovav and Paul Gray. "Managing Academic E-Journals;" https://cacm.acm.org/research/managing-academic-e-journals.

9. *Publishing Research Quarterly.* "Fees and Funding: Article Processing Charges (APCs);" https://link.springer.com/journal/12109/how-to-publish-with-us#Fees%20and%20Funding. Also see Rebecca Lea Morris. "Humanities Scholars Can Make Their Papers Open Access Now;" https://www.insidehighered.com/views/2022/04/13/humanities-scholars-can-act-now-go0open-access-opinion. Jennifer Ulz. "Open Access Publishing For Humanities Researchers;" https://www.editage.com/insights/open-access-publishing-for-humanities-researchers. Martin Paul Eve. "Digital Scholarly Journals Are Poorly Preserved: A Study of 7 Million Articles;" https://www.nature.com/articles/d41586-024-00616-5. Sarah Wild. "Millions of Papers At Risk of Disappearing From the Planet;" *Nature 627*(March 14, 2024): 256.

10. Nancy Maron, Charlotte Mulhern, Daniel Rossman, and Kimberly Schmelzinger. "The Costs of Publishing Monographs: Toward A Transparent Methodology;" https://sr.ithaka.org/publications/the-costs-of-publishing-monographs.
11. Ibid.
12. Ibid.
13. Ibid. Some of the university presses that provided data to the authors included Baylor, Johns Hopkins, Arizona, Arkansas, and Nebraska. Also see Erin Bartram. "How Much Money Do Historians Make From Their Writing?" https://contingentmagazine.org/2019/03/17/mailbag-2. Nancy Maron. "TOME Stakeholder Value Assessment;" https://doi.org/10.29242/report.tome2023.
14. Laura Brown, Maya Dayan, Brenna McLoughlin, Roger C. Schoenfeld, John Sherer, and Erich van Rijn. "Print Revenue and Open Access Monographs;" https://www.uploads/2023/09/AUP-sr-report-print-revenue-and-open-access-monographs=091923.pdf. Also see Hannah Lindy Herlich. "Transfer of Research Through Academic Publishing and the Use of OA Resources: A Survey," *Internet Reference Services Quarterly* *24*, 3–4(2019): 69–87. Laura Brown. "University Presses in the Age of Covid-19, Part 2;" https://sr-ithaka.org/blog/university-presses-in-the-age-of-covid-19-part-2.
15. Scott Jaschik. "More Humanities Books: Study Finds Increase in Number of New Titles—And Their Share of All New Scholarly Books;" https://www.insidehighered.com/news/2015/12/07/durvey-finds-growth-number-humanities-books-being-published.
16. Carl Straumsheim. "The Changing Monograph Market: Study Suggests University Presses Are Publishing Fewer Books in the Humanities. Experts Say the Publishing Industry Is Facing More significant Changes;" https://www.insidehighered.com/news/2017/02/20/study-suggests-university-presses-publish-fewer-humanities-books. Also see the Association of University Presses. "Reflecting on Five Years of Open Access Book Publishing: Successes, Lessons, and Next Step for TOME;" https://aupresses.org/events/reflecting-on-five-years-of-open-access-book-publishing-successes-lessons-and-next-steps-for-tome.
17. Rick Anderson. "How Important Are Library Sales to University Presses? One Case study;" https://scholarlykitchen.sspnet.org/2014/06/23/how-important-are-library-sales-to-the-university=press-one-case-study. Also see Cynthia Hudson Vitale and Judy Ruttenberg. "Invest in open Association of research Libraries: U.S. University member Expenditures on Services, Collections, Staff, and Infrastructure in Support of Open Scholarship;" https://www.arl.org/wp-content/uploads/2022/11/investments-in open.pdf.

18. Elizabeth A. Jones and Paul N. Courant. "Monographic Purchasing Trends in Academic Libraries: Did the 'Serials Crisis' Really Destroy the University Press?" *Journal of Scholarly Publishing 46*, 1(October 2014): 43–70.

19. Margaret Renld. "University Presses Are Keeping American Literature Alive;" https://nytimes.com/2022/11/14/opinion/university-presses-american-literature.

20. Peter Berkery and Annette Windhorn. "The Ethical Imperative of the University Press;" https://gwpress.manifoldapp.org/read/the-ethical-imperative-of-the-universioty-press/section/1d4a287a-50e3-4f1f-b8fe-ef31c756d427. Also see Anthony Cond and Jane Bunker. "Policy-making and the Future of scholarly Monographs;" https://digitaldigest.ip.hcommons.org/2024/04/25/policy-making-and-the-future-of-scholarly-monographs.

21. The Executive Council of the Modern Language Association (MLA). "Statement in Support of University Presses;" https://mla.org/Resources/Advocacy/Executive-Council/2019/Statement-in-Support-of-University-Presses.

22. Stanford University. "Finances-Stanford Facts;" https://facts.stanford.edu/administration/finances.

23. Alexander C. Kafka. "Proposed Cut of Stanford U. Press's Subsidy Sparks Outrage;" https://save-sup.org/files/articles/che/2019.4.26-outrage.pdf.

24. Association of University Presses. "Association Stands in Support of Stanford University Press;" https://aupresses.org/news/association-stands-in-support-of-stanford-university-press.

25. Paxton Scott. "Faculty Senate Discusses Consequences of Tight Budget, Graduate Student Affordability;" https://stanforddaily.co/2019/04/26/faculty-senate-discusses-cnsequences-of-tight-budget-graduate-student-affordability.

26. Ilya Somin. "University Presses Shouldn't Have to Make a Profit," *The Atlantic*, May 11, 2019, p. 9.

27. Alexander C. Kafka. "Facing Blowback, Stanford Partly Reverses Course and Pledges Press Subsidy for One More Year;" https://www.chronicle.com/article/facing-blowback-stanford-partly-reverses-course-and-pledges-press-subsidy-for-one-more-year. Also see Scott Jaschik. "Reprieve at Stanford;" https://www.insidehigjhered.com/news/2019/05/01/stanford-backs-down-year-ending-support-university-press. Karin Wulf. "Stanford University Press and the Wrong Lesson of the Humanities;" https://scholarlykitchen.sspnet.org/2019/06/24/stanford-university-press-and-the-wrong-lesson-of-the-humanities.

28. Carl Straumsheim. "Pressing Challenges: Amid Declining Book Sales, University Presses Search For New Ways to Measure Success;" https://

www.insidehighered.com/news/2016/08/01/amid-declining-book-sales-university-presses-search-new-ways-measure-success. Also see Scott Sherman. "University Presses Under Fire;" https://www.thenation.com/article/archive/university-presses-under-fire. Alison Mundditt. "The Past, Present, and Future of American Presses: A View From the Left Coast;" https://onlinelibrary.wiley.com/doi/full/10.1002/leap.1047.

29. Robert H. Townsend. "A Survey of Tenure Practices in History: Departments Indicate Books Are Key and Success Rates for Tenure High;" https://www.historians.org/research-and-publications/perspectives-on-history/february-2004/a-survey-of-tenure-practices-in-history. Also see Sarah Jones Weicksel. "AHA Today: Changing the Narrative: 'The State of the Humanities in the United States;" https://www.historians.org/research-and-publications/perspectives-on-history/january-2018/changing-the-narrative-the-state-and-future-of-the-humanities-in-the-ubnited-states. Patricia Oman. "The Humanities Model Is In Trouble," *Middle West Review 10*, 2(Spring 2024): 143–149.

30. Donald A. Barclay. "Academic Print Books Are Dying. What's the Future?" https://theconversation.com/academic-print-books-are-dying-whats-the-future. Also see Craig Lambert. "The 'Wild West' of Academic Publishing: The Troubled Present and Promising Future of Scholarly Communication;" http://www.harvardmagazine.com/2014/12/the-wild-west-of-academic-publishing.

31. Raym Crow. "A Rational System for Funding Scholarly Monographs: A White Paper Prepared for the AAU-ARL Task Force on Scholarly Communications;" https://www.arl.org/wp-content/uploads/2012/11/aau-arl-white-paper-rational-system-for-funding-scholarly-monographs-2012.pdf.

32. Philip Shaw, Angus Phillips, and Maria Bajo Gutierez. "The Death of the Monograph;" https://doi.org/10.1007/s12109-022-09885-2.

33. *Statistical Abstract of the United States 2024*; https://statabs-proquest-com.avoserv2.library.fordham.edu/statab/sa/index.html;JSESSIONIDE XT=587A43D0AFEB16DF1BBC15A5FE7FAD96.

34. Michelle Faverio and Andrew Perrin. "Three-in-Ten Americans Now Read E-Books:' https://www.pewresearch.org/short-reads/2022/01/06/three-in-ten-americans-now-read-e-books. Also see Tracy Bergstrom, Oya Y. Rieger, and Roger C. Schoenfeld. "The Second Digital Transformation of Scholarly Publishing;" https://sr.ithaka.org/wp-content/uploads/2024/01/SR-Report-Second-Digital-Transformation-of-Scholarly-Publishing-01292024.pdf. Avi Staiman. "10 Trends Observed Interviewing 10 Publishing Executives About the Future of Academic Books;" https://scholarlykitchen.sspnet.org/2023/05/23/10-trends-i-observed-interviewing-10-publishing-executives-about-the-future-of-academic-books.

35. Ted Levitt. "Marketing Myopia;" https://hbr.org/2004/07/marketing-myopia.
36. Ted Levitt. "People Don't Want Quarter-Inch Drills. They Want Quarter-inch Holes;" https://www.azquotes.com/author/21653-theodore_levitt.
37. Lindsay McKenzie. "Closing the Gap Between University Presses and Libraries;"https://www.insidehighered.com/news/2018/10/18/university-presses-take-control-ebook-distribution.
38. Ibid. Also see Charles Watkinson. "What Has the Covid-19 Pandemic Taught Us About Academic Book Publishing So far? A View from North America;" https://journals.publishing.umich.edu/jep/articles/id/1645.
39. MIT Press. "MIT Press Releases Direct-to-Open (D2O) Impact Report;" https://mitpress.mit.edu/mit-press-release-direct-to-open=d2o-impact-report. Also see Laureen Coffey. "A Viable Model for Open Access Publishing;" https://www.insidehighered.com/news/tech-innovation/digital-publishing/2024/05/28/mit-press-could-shift-higher-education. Lauren Coffey. "Open Access Books Help University Press Revenues, Study Finds;" https://www.insidehighered.com/news/quick-takes/2023/09/22/report-open-access-books-help-university-press-revenues. Laura Brown, Erich Van Run, Roger C, Schoenfeld, and John Sherer. "Open Access and Sales Revenue Can Co-Exist;" https://scholarlykitchen.sspnet.org/2023/09/21/open-access-sales-co-exist/#:~:text=OA%20titles%20can%20generate%20significant,revenue%20from%20their%20OA%20lists.
40. Allison Langham-Putrow, Caitlin Bakker, and Amy Riegelman. "Is the Open Access Citation Advantage Real? A Systematic Review of the Citation of Open Access and Subscription-Based Journals;" https://doi.org/10.1320/357e-ek33.
41. cOAlition S. "Towards Responsible Publishing;" https://www.coalition-s.org/towards-responsible-publishing. Also see Paul Longley Arthur and Lydia Hearn. "Open Scholarship in the Humanities;" https://www.blooms-bury.com/us/open-scholarship-in-the-humanities-9781350232273.
42. Steven Inchcombe. "Transformative Agreements Are Now the Key to Open Access;" https://www.timeshighereducation.com/blog/transfor mative-agreements-are-now-key-open-access. Also see Katherine Sanderson. "Who Will Pay for Scientific Publishing?" *Nature* 623(November 16, 2023): 472. Mariana Lenharo. "Will the Gates Foundation's Preprint-Centric Policy Help Open Access?" https://www.nature.com/articles/d41586-024-00996-8.
43. Christina Lembrecht. "If Authors Must Pay, Most humanities Scholarship Will Never Be Open Access;" https://www.timeshighereducation.com/blog/if-authors-must-pay-most-humanities-scholarsip-will-never-be-

open-access. Also see Nicholas Tampio. "The Problem With Making All Academic Research Free;" https://www.bostonglobe.com/2024/03/25/opinion/open-access-academic-research. Rick Anderson. "Where Did the Open Access Movement Go Wrong? An Interview With Richard Poynder;" https://scholarlykitchen.sspnet.org/2023/12/07/where-did-the-open-access-movement-go-wrong-an-intyerview-with-richard-poynder.

44. Loren B. Byrne. "Authors From Wealthy Countries Cannot All Pay Publishing Fees," *Nature 623* (January 2023): 472–473.

45. Leigh-Ann Butler, Lisa Matthias, Marc-Andre Simard, Philippe Mongeon, and Stafanie Haustein. "The Oligopoly's Shift to Open Access: How the Big Five Academic Publishers Profit From Article Processing Charges;" https://watermark.silverchair.com/qss_a_00272.pdf.

46. Fei Shu and Vincent Lariviere. "The Oligopoly of Open Access Publishing;" https://doi.org/10.1007/s11192-023-04876-2. Also see Jack Grove. "For-Profit Publishing Giants 'Big Winners' of Open Access Push;" https://www.timeshighereducation.com/news/profit-publishing-giants-big-winners-open-access-push.

47. Fordham University. "The Big Question: Why Study the Humanities?" https://now.fordham.edu/fordham-magazine/the-big-question-why-study-the-humanities. Also see Agnes Callard. "What Do the Humanities Do In A Crisis?" https://www.newyorker.com/culture/annals-of-inquiry/what-do-the-humanities-do-in-a-crisis. James Miller. "Introduction: The Future of Scholarly Knowledge in the Humanities," *Social Research 84*, 3(Fall 2017): 557–560.

48. bepress. "Digital Commons;" https://bepress.com/products/digital-commons.

49. The Nobel Prize. "Facts on the Nobel Prize in Literature;" https://www.nobelprize.org/prizes/facts/facts-on-the-nobel-prize-in-literature.

50. Chloe Berger. "The Rise of the English Major: BlackRock COO Wants to recruit Liberal Arts Analysts That Have Nothing To Do With Finance or Technology;"https://fortune.com/2024/05/17/black-rock-coo-robert-goldstein-english-history-liberal-arts-hiring. Also see Michael Thate. "The Humanities, Business, and the Question of Relevance (Humanities as a Resource and Inspiration for Humanizing Business);" https://link.springer.com/chapter/10.1007/978-3-031-33525-9_1.

51. Ryan Hogg. "IBM AI Chief Advises People Who Want A Tech Job in 2024 To Learn the Language and Creative Thinking Skills You Get With the Liberal Arts;" https://fortune.com/europe/2023/12/30/want-a-tech-job-in-2024-make-your-new-years-resolution-to-master-liberal-arts-and-language-ibm-ai-chief-says. Also see Brett Ingram and Lisa Cuklanz. "The Crisis in the Humanities and Its Relevance to Communication Studies;"

https://www.researchgate.net/publication/312178854_The_Crisis_in_
the_Humanities_and_its_Relevance_to_Communication_Studies.

52. Wilson Peden. "Why Critics Are Wrong About Liberal Arts Degrees;"
https://fortune.com/2015/11/13-liberal-arts-degrees-critics. Also see
Ashley Finley. "How College Contributes to Workforce Success;" https://
dgmg81phhvh63.cloudfront.net/content/user-photos/research/pdfs/
AACUEmployerReport2021.pdf. Also see Humanities Indicators.
"Employment Outcomes for Humanities Majors: State Profiles;" https://
www.amacad.org/publication/employment-outcomes-majors-state-
profiles.

53. U.S. Department of Labor (Labor). Bureau of Labor Statistics (BLS).
"What Can I Do With My Liberal Arts Degree?" https://bls.gov/career-
outlook/2017/article/liberal-arts.htm. Also see Karin Wulf. "Humanities
and Jobs Data: What's the Real Story?" https://scholarlykitchen.sspnet.
org/2023/12/14/humanities-and-jobs-data-whats-the-real-story.   The
Humanities Indicators. "State of the Humanities 2022: From Graduate
Education to the Workforce;" https://www.amacad.org/sites/default/
files/publication/downloads/2022_humanities-indicators_graduate-
education-workforce.pdf.

54. The National Endowment for the Humanities (NEH). "State and
Jurisdictional Humanities Councils;" https://www.neh.gov/about/state-
humanities-councils. Also see the National Endowment for the Humanities.
"Office of Federal/State Partnership;" https://www.neh.gov/about/
state-humanities-councils. Also see the State of Wyoming. "Wyoming
Humanities Announces Selections for National Book Festival;" https://
library.wyo.gov/wyoming-humanities-announces-selections-for-national-
book-festival.   Humanities   Commons.   "Humanities   Commons
Participating Organizations;" https://hcommons.org/societies.

55. The National Endowment for the Humanities. "Office of Digital
Humanities:" https://wwww.neh.gov/divisions/odh. Also see Claire
Battershill, Helen Southworth, Alice Staveley, Michael Widner, Elizabeth
Willson Gordon, Nicola Wilson. *Scholarly Adventures in Digital
Humanities: Making the Modernist Archives Publishing Project.* (Cham,
Switzerland: Palgrave Macmillan, 2017), pp. 17–94. Emily Twinch.
"Humanities Assessment 'Must Evolve for Digital Age';" https://ALLEA-
Report-Research-Assessment-in-e-Humanities.pdf. Dylan Ruediger and
Ruby MacDougall. "Are the Humanities ready for Data Sharing?" https://
sr.ithaka.org/wp-content/uploads/2023/03/SR-Issue-Brief-Data-
Sharing-in-the-Humanities-03062023.pdf.

56. David M. Berry. "What Are the Digital Humanities?" https://www.theb-
ritishacademy.ac.uk/blog/what-are-digital-humanities.

57. The National Endowment for the Humanities. "The Digital Humanities Advancement Grants;" https://www.neh.gov/grants/odh/digital-humanities-advancement-grants. Also see Luke Waltzer. "Digital Humanities and the 'Ugly Stepchildren' of American Higher Education;" https://dhdebates.gc.cuny.edu/read/untitled-88c11800-9446-469b-a3be-3fdb36bfbd1e/section/683df398-b766-41e0-9825-2247fc124f64.

58. The National Endowment for the Humanities. Office of Digital Humanities. "Digital Humanities Advancement Grants;" https://www.neh.gov/grants/odh/digital-humanities-advancement-grants#:~:text=The%20Digital%20Humanities%20Advancement%20Grants,public%20programming%20in%20the%20humanities.

59. The National Endowment for the Arts. "NEH Big Read;" https://www.arts.gov/initiatives/nea-big-read https://www.arts.gov/initiatives/nea-big-read.

60. The National Endowment for the Arts. "Announcing the 2024–2025 National Endowment for the Arts Big Read Communities;" https://www.arts.gov/news/press-releases/2024/announcing-2024-2025-national-endowment-arts-big-read-communities.

61. The Institute of Museum and Library Services. "Mission;" https://www.imts.gov.

62. Richard Drake. "The Crisis of University Research;" https://theamerican-scholarl.org/the-crisis-of-university-research.

63. Audrey Williams June. "Which Colleges Spent the Most Money on Research?" https://www.chronicle.com/article/which-colleges-spent-the-most-money-on-research.

64. Ibid.

65. Ibid.

66. Robert B. Townsend and Norman Bradburn. "The State of the Humanities Circa 2023;" https://doi.org/10.1162/DAED_a_01925.

67. Oddfrid Forland and Torgny Roxa. "Establishing Reward Systems for Excellence in Teaching—The Experience of Academic Pioneering A Reward System;" https://doi.org/10.1080/21568235.2023.2214713.

68. Christopher Mims. "AI Has been Massively Overhyped," *The Wall Street Journal*, June 1–2, 2024, pp. B1, B4.

69. The MLA [Modern Language Association] Ad Hoc Committee on the Future of Scholarly Publishing. "The Future of Scholarly Publishing," *Profession 2002* (New York: MLA, 2002), pp. 172–180.

70. Frank Lowney. "Understanding Why Scholarly Publishing Is A Cultural, Not Technological Issue;" https://www.smartbrief.com/original/understanding-why-academic-oublishing-today-cultural-not-technological.

71. Paul Reitter and Chad Wellmon. *Permanent Crisis: The Humanities in a Disenchanted Age* (Chicago: University of Chicago Press, 2021), pp. 221–252.

72. Helen Small. *The Value of the Humanities* (New York: Oxford University Press, 2016), pp. 125–174. Also see Adam Kirsch. "Stop Worrying About the 'Death' of the Humanities;" https://www.wsj.com/articles/stop-worrying-about-the-death-of-the-humanities-11556290279.   Deborah H. Holdstein. "Crisis? What Crisis? Defending the Humanities—And Literary Study," *Pedagogy 15*, 3(October 2015): 577–585.

73. Jeffrey Bilbro, Jessica Hooten Wilson, and David Henreckson (eds). *The Liberating Arts: Why We Need Liberal Arts Education* (Walden, NY: Plough Publishing House, 2023), pp. 2–39.

74. William D. Adams. "Martha C. Nussbaum Talks About the Humanities, Mythmaking, and International Development;" https://www.neh.gov/humanities/2017/spring/conversation/martha-c-nussbaum-talks-about-the-humanities-nythmakin-and-international-development.   Also see Martha C. Nussbaum. *Not for Profit: Why Democracy Needs the Humanities* (Princeton: Princeton University Press, 2017), pp. 11–73.

75. Yogi Berra. "The Future Isn't What It Used to be;" https://www.brainyquote.com/quotes/yogi_berra_102747. N.B. Yogi Berra is a member of the Baseball Hall of Fame and a former player with the New York Yankees.

BIBLIOGRAPHY

Abel, Richard and Lyman W. Newlin. *Scholarly Publishing: Books, Journals, Publishers, and Libraries in the Twentieth Century* (New York: Wiley, 2002).

Altbach, Philip G. *The Knowledge Context: Comparative Perspectives on the Distribution of Knowledge* (Albany, NY: State University of New York Press, 1987).

Altbach, Philip G. and Sheila McVey. *Perspectives on Publishing* (Lexington, MA: Lexington Books, 1976).

Alter, Robert. *The Pleasures of Reading in an Ideological Age* (New York: Simon & Schuster, 1989).

Amin, A. and Michael Mabe. "Impact Factors: Use and Abuse," *Perspectives in Publishing 1*(October 2000): 1–6.

Anglada, L. and N. Comellas. "What's Fair? Pricing Models in the Electronic Era," *Library Management, 23,* 4(April 2002): 227–233.

Arboleda, Amadio. "The Gutenberg Syndrome: An Illusion of International Research," *Journal of Scholarly Publishing 32,* 3(April 2001): 155–163

Arkenbout, Erwin, Frans Van Duk, and Peter Van Wuck. "Copyright in the Information Society: Scenario's and Strategies," *European Journal of Law and Economics 17 (2004):* 237–249.

Athill, Diana. *Stet: An Editor's Life* (New York: Grove, 2001).

Bagdikian, Ben H. *The Media Monopoly,* 6th ed. (Boston: Beacon Press, 2000).

Baker, Nicholas. *The Oxford University Press and the Spread of Learning: 1478–1978* (Oxford: Clarendon Press, 1978).

© The Author(s), under exclusive license to Springer Nature
Switzerland AG 2024
A. N. Greco, *Scholarly Publishing in the Humanities, 2000–2024,*
Marketing and Communication in Higher Education,
https://doi.org/10.1007/978-3-031-66170-9

Baker, Nicholson. "The Author vs. The Library." *The New Yorker,* 14 (October 1996): 50–62.

Baker, Nicholson. *Double Fold: Libraries and the Assault on Paper* (New York: Random House, 2001).

Baldwin, Peter. *Athena Unbound: Why and How Scholarly Knowledge Should be Free for All* (Cambridge, MA: MIT Press, 2023).

Balkin, Richard. *A Writer's Guide to Book Publishing* (New York: Plume, 1994).

Baten, Joerg; van Zanden, Jan Luiten. "Book Production and the Onset of Modern Economic Growth," *Journal of Economic Growth 13,* 3(2008): 217.

Baye, Michael R. and John Morgan. "Information Gatekeepers on the Internet and the Competitiveness of Homogeneous Product Markets," *The American Economic Review* 91, 3(June 2001): 454–474.

Bell, Bill (Ed.), *Where is Book History?* (Toronto: University of Toronto Press, 2002).

Berg, Nathan. "Coping With Journal-Price Inflation: Leading Policy Proposals and the Quality-Spectrum," *Economics Bulletin 4,* 14(2002): 1–8.

Bide, Mark. "Adding Value in Electronic Publishing: Taking the Reader's Perspective," *Business Information Review* 19, 1 (March 2002): 55–60.

Bilbro, Jeffrey, Jessica Hooten Wilson, and David Henreckson (eds.). *The Liberating Arts: Why We Need Liberal Arts Education* (Walden, New York: Plough Publishing House, 2023).

Birkets, Sven. *The Gutenberg Elegies: The Fate of Reading in an Electronic Age* (Boston: Faber & Faber, 1994).

Björk, B.C. "The Hybrid Model for Open Access Publication of Scholarly Articles – A Failed Experiment? *Journal of the American Society for Information Sciences and Technology, 63,* 8 (2012), 1496–15.

Björk, B.C. "Have the 'Megajournals' Reached the Limits to Growth? *PeerJ, 3* (2015) (e981). https://doi.org/10.7717/peerj.981.

Björk, B.C., & Solomon, D. Developing an Effective Market for Open Access Article Processing Charges;" Wellcome Trust, London, United Kingdom: Report http://www.wellcome.ac.uk/stellent/groups/corporatesite/@policy_communications/documents/web_document/wtp055910.pdf.

Bjork, B.C., & Solomon, D. "Article Processing Charges in OA Journals – Relationship Between Price and Quality. *Scientometrics, 103,* 2 (2015), 373–385.

Björk, B.C., M. Laakso, P. Welling, and P. Paetau. " Anatomy of Green Open Access," *Journal of the Association for Information Science and Technology, 65,* 2 (2014), 237–250.

Black, M.H. *Cambridge University Press: 1584–1984* (Cambridge, England: Cambridge University Press, 1984).

Boldrin, Michel and David Levine. "The Case Against Intellectual Property" The *American Economic Review* 92, 2(May 2002): 209–212.

Bonn, Thomas L. *Heavy Traffic and High Culture: New American Library as Literary Gatekeeper in the Paperback Revolution* (Carbondale, IL: Southern Illinois University Press, 1989).

Bonn, Thomas L. *Undercover: An Illustrated History of American Mass Market Paperbacks* (New York: Penguin, 1982).

Bontis, Nick and Alexander Serenko. "A Follow-Up Ranking of Academic Journals," *Journal of Knowledge Management 13*, 1 (2009): 16–26.

Bornmann, L, R. Mutz, and H-D Daniel. "Gender Differences in Grant Peer Review: A Meta-analysis," *Journal of Informetrics 1*, 3 (2007): 226–38.

Bourdieu, Pierre. "The Production of Belief: Contribution to an Economy of Symbolic Goods," *Media, Culture & Society 2*, 3 (1980): 261–293.

Bourdieu, Pierre. *Homo Academicus* (Stanford, CA: Stanford University Press 1988).

Bourdieu, Pierre. *Practical reason: On the theory of action.* Stanford, CA: Stanford University Press, 1998.

Bourdieu, Pierre. The rules of art: Genesis and structure of the literary field. Stanford, CA: Stanford University Press, 2006.

Bourdieu, Pierre. Symbolic capital and social classes. *Journal of Classical Sociology 13*, 2 (2013): 292–302. https://doi.org/10.1177/1468795X12468736.

Bowles, Gloria. "'Feminist Scholarship' and 'Women's Studies': Implications for University Presses," *The Journal of Scholarly Publishing 19*, 3 (April 1988): 163–168.

Brynjolfsson, Eric and Michael Smith. "Frictionless Commerce? A Comparison of Internet and Conventional Retailers," *Management Science 46*, 4(April 2000): 563–585.

Brynjolfsson, Erik and Michael D. Smith. "The Great Equalizer? Consumer Choice Behavior At Internet Shopbots." Working Paper MIT Sloan School of Management (July 2000b): 1–63.

Burchfield, Robert. "The Oxford English Dictionary and the State of the Language," *The Journal of Scholarly Publishing* 19, 3(April 1988): 169–178.

Burlingame, Roger. *Of Making Many Books: A Hundred Years of Reading, Writing, and Publishing.* University Park, PA: Pennsylvania State University Press, 1997.

Cameron, Samuel. "Cultural Economics, Books, and Reading," *Journal of Cultural Economics.* 2019; https://doi.org/10.1007/s/10824-019-09365-0.

Campbell, Margaret. "Perceptions of Price Unfairness: Antecedents and Consequences," *Journal of Marketing Research 36*, 2(1999): 187–199.

Campbell-Kelly, Martin and Garcia Swartz, Daniel D. "From Products to Services: The Software Industry in the Internet Era," *Business History Review 81*, 4(2007): 735–766.

Caplette, Michele. *Women in Publishing: A Study of Careers in Organizations.* Ph.D. dissertation, SUNY at Stony Brook, 1981.

Caro, Robert A. "Sanctum Sanctorum for Writers," *New York Times,* May 19, 1995, C1, C25.

Cerf, Bennett. *At Random: The Reminiscences of Bennett Cerf.* New York: Random House, 1977.

Childress, Clayton. *Under the Cover: The Creation, Production, and Reception of a Novel.* Princeton: University Press, 2017.

Chevalier, Judith A. and Austan Goolsbee. "Measuring Prices and Price Competition Online: Amazon and Barnes and Noble." Yale International Center for Finance. Working Paper # 02–23 (June 2002): 1–25.

Chong, Phillipa K. *Inside the Critics' Circle: Book Reviewing in Uncertain Times.* Princeton: Princeton University Press, 2020.

Christensen, Clayton M. *The Innovator's Dilemma: The Revolutionary Book That Will Change the Way You Do Business.* New York: HarperCollins, 2011.

Clay, Karen, Ramayya Krishnan, Eric Wolff, and Danny Fernandes. "Does A Seller's Ecommerce Reputation Matter? Evidence from eBay Auctions." The *Journal of Industrial Economics, 50,* 3 (September 2002): 351–367.

Clay, Karen, Ramayya Krishnan, and Eric Wolff. "Prices and Price Dispersion on the Web: Evidence from the Online Book Industry," *Journal of Industrial Economics 49,* 4(December 2001): 521–539.

Clerides, Sofronis K. "Pricing, Product Selection, and Consumer Choice in a Durable Good Market: The Book Publishing Industry," Ph. D. dissertation, Yale University, 1998.

Commins, Dorothy. *What Is An Editor? Saxe Commins At Work.* Chicago: University of Chicago Press, 1978.

Conaway, James. *America's Library: The Story of the Library of Congress, 1800–2000.* New Haven, CT: Yale University Press, 2000.

Coser, Lewis A., Charles Kadushin, and Walter W. Powell. *Books: The Culture and Commerce of Publishing.* Chicago: University of Chicago Press, 1985a.

Crider, Allen Billy. *Undercover: An Illustrated History of American Mass Market Paperbacks.* New York: Penguin, 1982a.

Crider, Allen Billy (Eds.), *Mass Market Publishing in America.* Boston: G.K.Hall & Co., 1982b.

Chowdhury, Gobinda. "Carbon Footprint of the Knowledge Sector: What's the Future?" *Journal of Documentation 66,* 6 (2010): 934–946. https://doi.org/10.1108/00220411011087878.

Clark, Allen, Jill Singleton-Jackson, and Ron Newsom. "Journal Editing: Managing the Peer Review Process for Timely Publication of Articles," *Publishing Research Quarterly 16,* 3 (2000): 62–71.

Conley, John P. and Myrna Wooders. "But What Have You Done For Me Lately? Commercial Publishing, Scholarly Communication, and Open-Access," *Economic Analysis & Policy 39,* 1(March 2009): 71–87.

Coser, Lewis A., Charles Kadushin, and Walter W. Powell. *Books: The Culture and Commerce of Publishing.* Chicago: University of Chicago Press, 1985b.

Dalton, Margaret Stieg. "The Publishing Experiences of Historians," *Journal of Scholarly Publishing 39,* 3(2008): 197–240.

Daum, Meghan. "Life On the Loaf: Two Weeks at the Bread Loaf Writer's Conference," *The New York Times Book Review,* 11 June 1995, 3, 46–47.

Davenport, Thomas H. and Jeanne G. Harris. "What People Want (and How to Predict It)," *MIT Sloan Management Review 50,* 2(2009): 22.

Davidson, Cathy N.(Ed.), *Reading in America: Literature and Social History.* Baltimore, MD: Johns Hopkins University Press, 1989.

Davidson, Cathy N. "The Futures of Scholarly Publishing," *Journal of Scholarly Publishing 35,* 3(April 2004): 129–142.

Davis, Kenneth C. *Two-Bit Culture: The Paperbacking of America.* Boston, MA: Houghton Mifflin Company, 1984.

Davis, Lee. "Intellectual Property Rights, Strategy, and Policy," *Economic Innovation and New Technology 13,*5 (2004): 399–415.

Diamond, Arthur M., Jr. *Open to Creative Destruction: Sustaining Innovative Dynamism.* New York: Oxford University Press, 2019.

De Los Santos, Babur, and Matthijs R. Wildenbeest. "E-Book Pricing and Vertical Restraints," *Quantitative Marketing and Economics, 15,* 2(2017), 85–122.

Derricourt, Robin. *An Author's Guide to Scholarly Publishing.* Princeton: Princeton University Press, 1996.

De Vany, Arthur and David Walls. "Bose-Einstein Dynamics and Adaptive Contracting in the Motion Picture Industry," *Economic Journal 106, 439(November* 1996): 1493–1514.

Di Leo, Jefferey E. "The Politics of Subventions: Crisis in the Humanities II," *American Book Review 52,* 5(July-August 2011): 2.

Dinlersoz, Emin M.; Li Han. "The Shipping Strategies of Internet Retailers: Evidence from Internet Book Retailing," *Quantitative Marketing and Economics 4,* 4(2006): 407–438.

DORA [Declaration on Research Assessment]. "San Francisco Declaration on Research Assessment;" https://sfdora.org/read.

Downs, Robert B. and Ralph E. McCoy. *The First Freedom Today: Critical Issues Relating to Censorship and to Intellectual Freedom.* Chicago: American Library Association, 1984.

Droegemeier, Kelvin K. *Demystifying the Academic Research Enterprise: Becoming a Successful Scholar in a Complex and Competitive Environment.* Cambridge, MA: MIT Press, 2023.

Drucker, Peter. *Management: Tasks, Responsibilities, Practices.* New York: Harper & Row, 1974.

Edlin, Aaron S. and Daniel L. Rubinfeld. "Competition Policy for Journals [Dagger]: The Bundling of Academic Journals," *The American Economic Review 95*, 2 (2005): 441–446.

Edlin, A. and Rubinfeld, D. (2004). Exclusion Or Efficient Pricing: The "Big Deal" Bundling of Academic Journals;" http://works.bepress.com/aaron_edlin/37/

Edmonds, Leslie. "The Treatment of Race in Picture Books for Young Children," *Book Research Quarterly* 2(Fall 1986): 30–41.

Eisenstein, Elizabeth L. The *Printing Press as an Agent of Change*, 2 Vols. New York: Cambridge University Press, 1979.

Englund, Sheryl A. "A Dignified Success: Knopf's Translation and Promotion of *The Second Sex*," *Publishing Research Quarterly* 10(Summer 1994): 5–18.

Epstein, Jason. *Book Business: Publishing Past, Present, and Future.* New York: W.W. Norton, 2001.

Epstein, Jason. "The Decline and Rise of Publishing," *New York Review of Books* (March 1, 1990): 8–12.

Estelle, L. "Unravelling the True Cost of Publishing In Open Access;" http://www.jisc.ac.uk/blog/unravelling-the-true-cost-of-publishing-in-open-access-15-dec-2014.

Ezell, Margaret J.M. *Social Authorship and the Advent of Print: The Editor's Advice to Writers.* Baltimore, MD: Johns Hopkins University Press, 2000.

Faria, João Ricardo and Rajeev K. Goel. "Returns to Networking in Academia," *Netnomics: Economic Research and Electronic Networking 11*, 2 (2010): 103–117.

Fish, Stanley. "Will the Humanities Save Us? https://opinionator.blogs.nytimes.com/2008/01/06/will-the-humanities-save-us./

Flaherty, Colleen. "Early Journal Submission Data Suggest COVID-19 Is Tanking Women's Research Productivity;" www.insidehighered.com/news/2020/04/21/early-journal-submission-data-suggest-covid-19-tanking-womens-research-productivity.

Franklin, Sara B. *The Editor: How Publishing Legend Judith Jones Shaped Culture in America.* New York: Atria Books, 2024.

Fruge, August. *A Skeptic Among Scholars: August Fruge on University Publishing.* Berkeley, CA: University of California Press, 1993.

Garfield, Eugene and I.H. Shaw. "New Factors in the Evaluation of Scientific Literature Through Citation Indexing," *American Documentation 14*, 3(July 1983): 195.

Germano, William. *Getting it Published: A Guide for Scholars and Anyone Else Serious About Serious Books.* Chicago: University of Chicago Press, 2001a.

Germano, William. "Surviving the Review Process," *The Journal of Scholarly Publishing, 33*, 1 (October 2001b): 53–69.

Ghose, Anindya, Michael D. Smith, and Rahul Telang. "Internet Exchanges for Used Books: An Empirical Analysis for Welfare Implications." Working Paper; Carnegie Mellon University, 2004.

Gottlieb, Robert. *Avid Reader: A Life*. New York: Farrar, Straus and Giroux, 2016.

Graham, Andrew. "The Assessment: Economics of the Internet," *Oxford Review of Economic Policy* 17, 2 (2001): 145–158.

Graham, Gordon and Richard Abel (Eds.), *The Book in the United States Today*. New Brunswick, NJ: Transaction Publishers, 1996.

Graubard, Stephen R. and Paul LeClerc (Eds.), *Books, Bricks, & Bytes*. New Brunswick, NJ: Transaction Publishers, 1998.

Greco, Albert N. "The Changing Market for U.S. Book Exports and Imports," in *The Bowker Annual 2004: 49ʰ edition*, ed. Dave Bogart. Medford, NJ: Information Today, Inc., 2004.

Greco, Albeit N. "Domestic Consumer Expenditures for Consumer Books: 1984–1994," *Publishing Research Quarterly* 14(Fail 1998): 12–28.

Greco, Albert N. "The First Amendment, Freedom of the Press, and the Issue of 'Harm:' A Conundrum for Publishers," *Publishing Research Quarterly* 11(Winter 1995/1996a): 39–57.

Greco, Albert N. 'The General Reader Market for University Press Books in the United States, 1990–1999, With Projections for the Years 2000 Through 2004," *The Journal of Scholarly Publishing* 32, 2(January 2001): 61–85.

Greco, Albert N. "The Impact of Horizontal Mergers and Acquisitions on Corporate Concentration in the U.S. Book Publishing Industry, 1989–1994" *The Journal of Media Economics* 12, 3(Fall 1999): 165–180.

Greco, Albert N. "International Book Title Output: 1990–1999," in *The Bowker Annual 2000: 45th Edition*, Dave Bogart (Ed.), New Providence, NJ: R.R. Bowker, 2000a, pp. 528–531.

Greco, Albert N. "Market Concentration in the U.S. Consumer Book Industry: 1995–1996," *The Journal of Cultural Economics* 24, 4(November 2000b): 321–336.

Greco, Albert N. "The Market for Consumer Books in the U.S.: 1985–1995'" *Publishing Research Quarterly* 13(Spring 1997): 3–40.

Greco, Albert N. (Ed.), *The Media and Entertainment Industries*. Boston: Allyn & Bacon, 2000c.

Greco, Albert N. "Mergers and Acquisitions in Publishing, 1984–1988: Some Public Policy Issues," *Book Research Quarterly* 5(Fall 1989): 25–44.

Greco, Albert N. "Mergers and Acquisitions in the U.S. Book Publishing Industry: 1960–1989," in *International Book Publishing: An Encyclopedia*, Philip G. Altbach and Edith S. Hoshino (Eds.), New York: Garland Publishing, Inc., 1995, pp. 229–242.

Greco, Albert N. "Publishing Economics: Mergers and Acquisitions within the Publishing Industry 1980–1989," in *Media Economics: Theory and Practice*, Alison Alexander, James Owers, and Rodney Carveth (Eds.), Hillside, NJ: Lawrence Erlbaum Associates, 1993, 205–224.

Greco, Albert N. "Shaping the Future: Mergers, Acquisitions, and the U.S. Publishing, Communications, and Mass Media Industries, 1990–1995," *Publishing Research Quarterly 12*(Fall 1996b): 5–15.

Greco, Albert N. "U. S. Book Returns, 1984–1989," *Publishing Research Quarterly* 8(Fall 1992): 46–61.

Gross, Gerald. *Editors on Editing*. New York: Grove Press, 1993.

Gu, Xian, P.K. Kannan, and Liye Ma. "Selling the Premium in Freemium," *Journal of Marketing* 82, 6(2018): 10–27.

Hackett, Alice Payne and James Henry Burke. *80 Years of Best Sellers, 1895–1975*. New York, R.R. Bowker, 1975.

Hall, Frania. *The Business of Digital Publishing: An Introduction to the Digital Book and Journal Industries,* (2nd ed). London: Routledge, 2022.

Hall, James, W. *Hit Lit: Cracking the Code of Twentieth Century's Biggest Bestsellers.* New York: Random House, 2012.

Hall, Max. *Harvard University Press: A History.* Cambridge, MA: Harvard University Press, 1986.

Hansmann, Henry and Reinier Kraakman. "Hands-Tying Contracts: Book Publishing, Venture Capital Financing, and Secured Debt," *Journal of Law, Economic, and Organization 8,3*(1992): 628–655.

Harnad, S., Brody, T., Vallieres, F., Carr, L., Hitchcock, S., Gingras, Y., Oppenheim, C., et al. "The Access/Impact Problem and the Green and Gold Roads to Open Access," *Serials Review 30*, 4 (2004), 310–314.

Harnum, Bill. "The Characteristics of the Ideal Acquisition Editor," *The Journal of Scholarly Publishing* 32, 4(July 2001): 182–188.

Hart, James D. *The Popular Book: A History of America 's Literary Taste*. New York: Oxford University Press, 1950.

Hartwick, Elisabeth. "The Decline of Book Reviewing;" https://harpers.org/archieve/1959/10/the-decline-of-book-reviewing.

Haughey, Jim and Deborah Selsky. "The Economic Context of Book Publishing," *Publishing Research Quarterly* 6(Winter 1990/1991): 62–65.

Hayes, Robert H. and William J. Abernathy. "Managing Our Way to Economic Decline," *Harvard Business Review* 58 (July-August 1980): 67–77.

Henderson, Bill. *The Art of Literary Publishing: Editors on Their Craft.* Wainscott, NY: Pushcart Press, 1980.

Henry, Robert W. *Comstockery in America: Patterns of Censorship and Control.* Boston, MA: Beacon Press, 1960.

Herubel, Jean-Pierre V.M. "Historical Scholarship, Periodization, Themes and Specialization: Implications for Research and Publication," *Journal of Scholarly Publishing 39*, 2(2008): 144–155.

Hexter, J.H. "Publish or Perish;" https://search.proquest.com/docview/129 8134010?accountid=14511

Hinckley, Karen and Barbara Hinckley. *American Best Sellers: A Reader's Guide to Popular Fiction.* Bloomington, IN: Indiana University Press, 1989.

Horowitz, Irving Louis. *Communicating Ideas: The Crisis of Publishing in a Post-Industrial Society.* New Brunswick, NJ: Transaction Publishers, 1992.

Houghton, John; Sheehan, Peter. "Estimating the Potential of Open Access to Research Findings," *Economic Analysis and Policy* 39, 1(2009): 127–142.

Hutchinson, Ann M. *Editing Women.* Toronto: University of Toronto Press, 1998.

Hutton, Frankie. *The Early Black Press in America, 1827 to 1860.* Westport, CT: Greenwood, 1992.

Hyland, K. *Academic Publishing: Issues and Challenges in the Construction of Knowledge.* Oxford: Oxford University Press, 2015.

Jacso, Peter. "The h-Index, h-Core Citation Rate, and the Bibliometric Profile of the Scopus Database," *Online Information Review 35*, 3(2011): 492–501.

Jasco, Peter. "The Plausibility of Computing the h-Index of Scholarly Productivity and Impact Using Reference Enhanced Databases," *Online Information Review 32*, 2(2008): 266–283.

Jasco, Peter. "The Pros and Cons of Computing the h-Index Using Web of Science," *Online Information Review 32*, 5(2009): 673–688.

Jeanneret, Marsh. *God and Mammon: Universities as Publishers.* Urbana and Chicago: University of Illinois Press, 1990.

Jones, Candace. "Creative Industries," *Administrative Science Quarterly 46*, 3(September 2001): 567–571.

Jones M.J., T. Brinn, and M. Pendleburry. "Journal Evaluation Methodologies: A Balanced Response," *Omega, International Journal of Management Science 24*, 5(1996): 607–612.

Joyce, Donald Franklin. *Gatekeepers of Black Culture: Black-Owned Book Publishing in the United States,* 1817–1981. Westport, CT: Greenwood Press, 1983.

Kachka, Boris. *Hothouse: The Art of Survival and the Survival of Art at America's Most Celebrated Publishing House Farrar Straus and Giroux.* New York: Simon & Schuster, 2013.

Kahin, Brian and Hal R. Varian. (Eds.), *Internet Publishing and Beyond: The Economics of Digital Information and Intellectual Property.* Cambridge: MIT Press, 2000.

Kannan, P.K., Barbara Kline Pope, and Sanjay Jain. "Pricing Digital Content Product Lines: A Model and Application for the National Academies Press," *Marketing Science, 28*, 4(2009), 620–36.

Kazin, Alfred, Dan Lacy, and Ernest L. Boyer. *The State of the Book World, 1980: Three Talks Sponsored by the Center for the Book in the Library of Congress.* Washington, DC: Library of Congress, 1981.

Kernan, Alvin B., William G. Bowen, and Harold T. Shapiro. *What Happened to the Humanities?* Princeton: Princeton University Press, 1997.

Kim, Nancy S. "The Software Licensing Dilemma," *Brigham Young University Law Review 2008*, 4(2008): 1103–1165.

Kingston, Paul William and Jonathan R. Cole. *The Wages of Writing: Per Word, Per Piece, or Perhaps*. New York: Columbia University Press, 1986.

Klein, Benjamin, Andres V. Lerner, and Kevin Murphy. 'The Economics of Copyright 'Fair Use' in a Networked World," *The American Economic Review* 92, 2(May 2002): 205–208.

Knopf, Alfred A. *Publishing Then & Now: 1912–1964*. New York: New York Public Library, 1964.

Knopf, Alfred A. *Some Random Recollections*. New York: The Typophiles, 1949.

Korda, Michael. *Making the List: A Cultural History of the American Bestseller 1900–1999*. New York: Barnes & Noble Books, 2001.

Kranton, Rachael E. and Deborah F. Minehart. "A Theory of Buyer-Seller Networks," The *American Economic Review* 91, 3(June 2001): 485–508.

Kwak, Hyokjin, Richard J.Fox, and George M. Zinkhan. "What Products Can Be Successful Promoted and Sold Via the Internet?" *Journal of Advertising Research* 42, 1 (January/February 2002): 23–38.

Lal, Rajiv and Miklos Sarvary. "When and How is the Internet Likely to Decrease Price Competition?" *Management Science* 45(1999): 485–503.

Larivière, V., Haustein, S. and Mongeon, P. (2015). "The Oligopoly of Academic Publishers in the Digital Era;" https://doi.org/10.1371/journal.pone.0127502.

Levack, Kinley. "Pressing the POD Issue: The MIT Classics Series," *EContent 26*, 7(July 2003): 9.

Levitt, Theodore. "Marketing Myopia," *Harvard Business Review* 53 (September-October 1975): 26–37.

Lewis, Freeman, *A Brief History of Pocket Books*. New York: Pocket Books, 1967.

Lippitt, Mary Burner. "Six Priorities That Make A Great Strategic Decision," *The Journal of Business Strategy 24*, 1(2003): 21–25.

Litan, Robert E. and Alice M. Rivlin. "Projecting the Economic Impact of the Internet," *The American Economic Review* 91, 2(May 2001): 313–317.

Long, Elizabeth. *The American Dream and the Popular Novel*. Boston: Routledge & Kegan Paul, 1985.

Lorenzen, Mark and Frederiksen, Lars. "Why Do Cultural Industries Cluster? Localization, Urbanization, Products and Projects," *New Horizons in Regional Science*, (2008): 155–179.

Lucas, Henry C., Jr. *Strategies for Electronic Commerce and the Internet*. Cambridge: MIT Press, 2002.

Lukianoff, Greg and Rickki Schlott. *The Canceling of the American Mind*. New York: Simon & Schuster, 2023.

Mabe, Michael A. "The Growth and Number of Journals," *Serials 16*, 2(2003): 191–197.

Machlup, Fritz and Kenneth Leeson. *Information Through the Printed Word*, Vol. 1, *Book Publishing*. New York: Praeger, 1978.

Mackenzie Owen, John. "The New Dissemination of Knowledge: Digital Libraries and Institutional Roles in Scholarly Publishing," *Journal of Economic Methodology 9*, 3(2002a): 275–288.

Mackenzie Owen, John. "The New Dissemination of Knowledge: Digital Libraries and Institutional Roles in Scholarly Publishing," *Journal of Economic Methodology 9*, 3(2002b): 275–288.

Maharg, Paul and Nigel James Duncan. "Black Box, Pandora's Box or Virtual Toolbox? An Experiment in a Journal's Transparent Peer Review on the Web," *International Review of Law, Computers, & Technology 21*, 2(2007): 109–128.

Manguel, Alberto. *A History of Reading*. New York: Penguin Books, 1997.

Marcum, Deanna and Roger C. Schoenfeld. *Along Came Google: A History of Library Digitization*. Princeton: Princeton University Press. 2021.

Markert, John. *Publishing Romance: A History of the Industry, 1940s to the Present*. Jefferson, North Carolina: McFarland & Co., 2016.

McCartan, Patrick. "Journals and the Production of Knowledge: A Publishing Perspective," *British Journal of Political Science 40*, 2 (2010): 237–248.

McCormack, Thomas. *The Fiction Editor: The Novel, and the Novelist*. New York: St. Martin's Press, 1988.

McGuigan, Glenn S. and Robert D. Russell. "The Business of Academic Publishing: A Strategic Analysis of the Academic Journal Publishing Industry and Its Impact on the Future of Scholarly Publishing," *Electronic Journal of Academic and Special Librarianship 9*, 3(Winter 2008): 1–11.

McGurl, Mark. *The Program Era: Postwar Fiction and the Rise of Creative Fiction*. Cambridge: Harvard University Press, 2011.

McLuhan, Marshall *The Gutenberg Galaxy*. Toronto: University of Toronto Press, 1962.

McLuhan, Marshall and Quentin Fiore. *The Medium Is the Message*. New York: Bantam Books, 1967.

McLuhan, Marshall and Eric McLuhan. *The New Science*. Toronto: University of Toronto Press, 1992.

McQuivey, James L. and Megan K.McQuivey. "Is It a Small Publishing World After All: Media Monopolization and the Children's Book Market" *Journal of Media Economics 11*, 4(1998): 35–48.

Meltzer, Franchise. *Hot Property: The Stakes and Claims of Literary Originality*. Chicago: University of Chicago Press, 1994.

Menaker, Dan. *My Mistake*. New York: HarperCollins, 2014.

Miller, Luke T., Alice Smith, and Elaine Labach. "Guidelines and Advice for Successful Publication Provided by Journal Editors," *American Journal of Business Education 3*, 3 (2010): 17–33.

Miller, James. "Introduction: The Future of Scholarly Knowledge in the Humanities," *Social Research: An International Quarterly 84*, 3(Fall 2017): 557–560.

Mizzaro, Stefano. "Quality Control in Scholarly Publishing: A New Proposal," *Journal of the American Society for Information Science and Technology 54*, 11(September 2003): 989–1005.

Moosa, I.A. *Publish or Perish: Perceived Benefits Versus Unintended Consequences.* Cheltenham, UK: Edward Elgar Publishing, 2018.

Monbiot, George. "Academic Publishers Make Murdoch Look Like A Socialist;" http://www.guardian.co.uk/commentisefree/2011/aug/29/academic-opublishers-murdoch.

Monbiot, George. "The Lairds of Learning;" http://www.monbiot.com/2011/08/29/the-lairds-of-learning.

Morton, Herbert C. *The Story of Webster's Third: Philip Gove's Controversial Dictionary and Its Critics.* New York: Cambridge University Press, 1994.

Mott, Frank L. *Golden Multitudes: The Story of Best Sellers in the United States.* New York: R.R. Bowker, 1947.

Moylan, Michele and Lane Stiles (Eds.), *Reading Books: Essays on the Material Text and Literature in America.* Amherst, MA: University of Massachusetts Press, 1996.

Narin, Francis and Mark P. Carpenter. "National Publication and Citation Comparisons," *Journal of the American Society for Information Science 26*, 2(March/April 1975): 80.

National Academies. *Electronic, Scientific, Technical, and Medical Journal Publishing and Its Implications.* Washington, DC: The National Academies, 2004; pages 1–74.

Nelson, Kristopher A. "The Impact of Government-Mandated Public Access to Biomedical Research: An Analysis of the New NIH Depository Requirements," http://ssrn.com/abstract=1147427.

Nicholas, David. "Scholarly and Professional Journals in the Digital Environment," *Records Management Journal 20*, 3(2010a): 291–300.

Nicholas, David, Paul Huntington, and Ian Rowlands. "Open Access Journal Publishing: The Views of Some of the World's Senior Authors," *Journal of Documentation 61*, 4 (2005): 497–519.

Nicholas, David. "Scholarly and Professional Journals in the Digital Environment," *Records Management Journal 20*, 3 (2010b): 291–300.

Norris, Michael and Charles Oppenheim. "The h-Index: A Broad Review of a New Bibliometric Indicator," *Journal of Documentation 66*, 5(2010): 681–705.

Northcott, Deryl and Simon Lincare. "Producing Spaces for Academic Discourse: The Impact of Research Assessment Exercises and Journal Quality Rankings," *Australian Accounting Review 20*, 1(March 2010): 38–54.

O'Brien, Geoffrey. *Hardboiled America: The Lurid Years of Paperbacks.* New York: Van Nostrand Reinhold, 1981.

Oguniesi, Tolu. "What Is Global Publishing Worth? A: €80 Billion;" http://publishingperspectives.com/2011/04/what-is-global-publishing-worth./

Packard, Ashley. "Copyright or Copy Wrong: An Analysis of University Claims to Faculty Work," *Communication and Law Policy 7* (Summer 2002): 275–316.

Parks, Robert P. "The Faustian Grip of Academic Publishing," *Journal of Economic Methodology 9*, 3(2002):317–335.

Parsons, Paul. *Getting Publishing: The Acquisition Process at University Presses.* Knoxville, TN: University of Tennessee Press, 1989.

Perkins, Maxwell E. *Editor to Author.* John Hall Wheelock (Ed.), New York: Charles Scribner's Sons, 1950.

Peters, Jean. "Book Industry Statistics from the R.R. Bowker Company," *Publishing Research Quarterly 8* (Fall 1992): 12–23.

Peterson, Clarence. *The Bantam Story: Thirty Years of Paperback Publishing.* New York: Bantam, 1975.

Pettegree, Andrew and Arthur der Weduwen. *The Library: A Fragile History.* New York: basic Books,2021.

Phillips, Owen R. and Lori J. Phillips. "The Market for Academic Journals," *Applied Economics 34*, 1(2002): 39–48.

Pinckney, Darryl. *Come Back in September: A Literary Education on West 67ᵗʰ Street Manhattan.* London: Picador, 2023

Plant, Arnold. "The Economic Aspects of Copyright in Books," *Economica 1*, 2(May 1934): 167–195.

Plumb, J.H. (ed.). *Crisis in the Humanities.* Middlesex, England: Pelican Books, 1964.

Pool, Ithiel de Sola. "The Culture of Electronic Print" *Daedalus* 111(Fall 1982): 17–32.

Pool, Ithiel de Sola. *Technologies of Freedom.* Boston: Harvard University Press, 1983.

Porter, Michael E. *Competitive Strategy: Techniques for Analyzing Industries and Competitors.* New York: Free Press, 1980.

Porter, Michael E. "The Five Competitive Forces That Shape Strategy,". *Harvard Business Review, 86*, 1(2008), 78–93.

Porter, Michael E. 1991. "Towards a Dynamic Theory of Strategy," *Strategic Management Journal 12*(1991): 95–117.

Porter, Michael E. and Scott Stern. "Innovation: Location Matters." *MIT Sloan Management Review 42*, 4(2001): 28–36.

Posner, Richard A. *Public Intellectuals: A Study of Decline.* Cambridge: Harvard University Press, 2001.

Powell, Walter W. "From Craft to Corporation: The Impact of Outside Ownership on Book Publishing," *in Individuals in Mass Media Organizations: Creativity and Constraint.* J.S. Ettema and D.C.Whitney (Eds.), Beverly Hills, CA: Sage, 1982.

Powell, Walter W. *Getting Into Print: The Decision Making Process in Scholarly Publishing.* Chicago: University of Chicago Press, 1985.

Pratt, Andy C. "Cultural Commodity Chains, Cultural Clusters, or Cultural Production Chains?" *Growth and Change 39,* 1(2008): 95–103.

Prosser, D. "From Here to There: A Proposed Mechanism for Transforming Journals from Closed to Open Access," *Learned Publishing, 16,* 3 (2003), 163–166.

Radway, Janice A. *A Feeling for Books: The Book-of-the-Month Club, Literary Taste, and Middle-Class Desire.* Capel Hill, NC: University of North Carolina Press, 1997.

Radway, Janice A. *Reading the Romance: Women, Patriarchy, and Popular Literature.* Chapel Hill, NC: University of North Carolina Press, 1984.

Rainer, R. Kelley and Mark D. Miller. "Examining Differences Across Journal Rankings," *Communications of the ACM 48,* 2 (February 2005a): 91–94.

Ramello, Giovanni Battista. "Copyright & Endogenous Market Structure: A Glimpse from the Journal Publishing Market," *Review of Economic Research on Copyright Issues, 7,* 1(2010a): 7–29.

Raustiala, Kai and Christopher Springman. "The Piracy Paradox Revisited," *Stanford Law Review 61,* 5(2009): 6–11. Samuelson, Pamela. "Copyright's Fair Use Doctrine and Digital Data" *Publishing Research Quarterly 11,* 1 (Spring 1995): 27–39.

Rainer, R. Kelley and Mark D. Miller. "Examining Differences Across Journal Rankings," *Communications of the ACM 48,* 2 (February 2005b): 91–94.

Ramello, Giovanni Battista. "Copyright & Endogenous Market Structure: A Glimpse from the Journal Publishing Market," *Review of Economic Research on Copyright issues 7,* 1(2010b): 7–29.

Raustiala, Kai and Christopher Springman. "The Piracy Paradox Revisited," *Stanford Law Review 61,* 5(2009): 6–11.

Reitter, Paul and Chad Wellmon. *Permanent Crisis: The Humanities in a Disenchanted Age.* Chicago: University of Chicago Press, 2021.

Remer, Rosalind. *Printers and Men of Capital: Philadelphia Book Publishers in the New Republic.* Philadelphia, PA: University of Pennsylvania Press, 1996.

Reskin, Barbara F. "Culture, Commerce, and Gender: The Feminization of Book Editing," In *Job Queues, Gender Queues: Explaining Women's Inroads into Male Occupations* Barbara F. Reskin and Patricia A. Roos (Eds.), Philadelphia, PA: Temple University Press, 1990.

Rose, Mark. *Authors and Owners: The Invention of Copyright.* Cambridge, MA: Harvard University Press, 1993.

Rosner, Charles. *The Growth of the Book Jacket.* Cambridge, MA: Harvard University Press, 1954.

Ross, Michael N. *Publishing in the Digital Age: How Business Can Thrive in a Rapidly Changing Environment*. London: Routledge, 2022.

Royal Historical Society. "Plan S and History;" journals. https://royalhistsoc.org/policy/publication-open-access/plan-s-and-history-journals./

Rutherford, Brett. "Print-on-Demand Here to Stay for Region's Successful Printers," *Printing News* (April 15, 2002): 24.

Samuelson, Pamela. "Copyright's Fair Use Doctrine and Digital Data" *Publishing Research Quarterly 11*, 1 (Spring 1995): 27–39.

Sargent, John. *Turning Pages: The Adventures and Misadventures of a Publisher*. New York: Arcade Publishing, 2023.

Schick, Frank L. *The Paperbound Book in America: The History of Paperbacks and Their European Background*. New York: R.R. Bowker, 1958.

Schiffrin, Andre. *The Business of Books: How International Conglomerates Took Over Publishing and Changed the Way We Read*. New York: Verso, 2000.

Schiffrin, Andre. "The Corporatization of Publishing," *The Nation* (June 3, 1996): 29–33.

Schiller, Herbert I. *Culture, Inc.: The Corporate Takeover of Public Expression*. New York: Oxford University Press, 1989.

Schreyer, Alice D. *The History of Books: A Guide to Selected Resources in the Library of Congress*. Washington, DC: Library of Congress/The Center for the Book, 1987.

Scribner, Charles, Jr. *In the Company of Writers: A Life in Publishing*. New York: Charles Scribner's Sons, 1990.

Scribner, Charles, Jr. *In the Web of Ideas: The Education of a Publisher*. New York: Charles Scribner's Sons, 1993.

Scribner III, Charles. *Scribners: Five Generations in Publishing*. Essex, CT: Lyons Press, 2023.

See, Carolyn. *Making a Literary Life*. New York: Random House, 2002.

Segran, E. "What Can You Do with a Humanities Ph.D., Anyway?" www.theatlantic.com/business/archive/2014/03/what-can-you-do-with-a-humanities-phd-anyway/359927.

Server, Lee. *Over My Dead Body: The Sensational Age of the American Paperback: 1945–1955*. San Francisco: Chronicle Books, 1994.

Shape, Leslie T. and Irene Gunther. *Editing Fact and Fiction: A Concise Guide to Book Editing*. New York: Cambridge University Press, 1994.

Shatzkin, Leonard. *In Cold Type: Overcoming the Book Crisis*. Boston: Houghton Mifflin, 1982.

Shavell, Steven and Tanquy van Ypersele. "Rewards Versus Intellectual Property Rights," *Journal of Law and Economics 44*, 2(2001): 525–547.

Shiller, Robert J. "Conversation, Information, and Herd Behavior," *Rhetoric and Human Behavior 85*, 2(1995): 181–185.

Schiller, Robert J. "From Efficient Market Theory to Behavioral Finance," *Journal of Economic Perspectives 17*, 1 (Winter 2003): 83–104.

Shiller, Robert J. "Human Behavior and the Efficiency of the Financial System," Yale University Cowles Discussion Paper (1998): 1–34.

Shiller, Robert J. *Irrational Exuberance.* Princeton: Princeton University Press, 2000.

Silverman, Al (Ed.), *The Book of the Month: Sixty Years of Books in American Life.* Boston, MA: Little Brown, 1986.

Sinykin, Dan. *Big Fiction: How Conglomeration Changed the Publishing Industry and American Literature.* New York: Columbia University Press, 2023.

Skillin, Marjorie and Robert M. Gay. *Words Into Type.* New York: Prentice-Hall, 1974.

Small, Helen. *The Value of the Humanities.* Oxford: Oxford University Press, 2013.

Smallwood, Christine. "A reviewer's Life: The Material Constraints of Writing Criticism;" https://yalereview.org/article/christne-smallwood-reviewers-life.

Smith, Anthony. *The Geopolitics of Information: How Western Culture Dominates the World.* New York: Oxford University Press, 1980.

Smith, Anthony. *The Politics of Information: Problems of Policy in Modern Media.* London: Macmillan, 1979.

Smith, Gordon V. and Russell L. Parr. *Valuation of Intellectual Property and Intangible Assets, 3rd ed.* New York: John Wiley & Sons, 2000.

Smith, Michael and Eric Brynjolfsson. "Consumer Decision-Making at an Internet Shopbot: Brand Still Matters," *The Journal of Industrial Economics* XLIX(December 2001): 541–558.

Smith, Roger H. (Ed.), *The American Reading Public: What It Reads, Why It Reads.* New York: R.R. Bowker, 1961.

Smith, Stanley. "Is An Article in a Top Journal a Top Article?" *Financial Management 33*, 4(Winter 2004): 133–149.

Snow, C.P. *The Two Cultures.* Cambridge: Cambridge University Press, 1998.

Snow, C.P. *The Two Cultures and the Scientific Revolution: The Rede Lecture.* New York: Cambridge University Press, 2012.

Solomon, D., Laakso, M., & Björk, B.C. *Converting Scholarly Journals to Open Access – A Review of Approaches and Experiences.* Harvard Library Office for Scholarly Communication: Report. http://nrs.harvard.edu/urn-3:HUL.InstRepos:27803834.

Solotaroff, Ted. *A Few Good Voices in My Head: Occasional Pieces on Writing, Editing, and Reading My Contemporaries.* New York: Harper & Row, 1987a.

Solotaroff, Ted. "The Literary-Industrial Complex," *New Republic* (June 8, 1987b): 28, 30–42, 44–45.

Staber, Udo. "Network Evolution in Cultural Industries," *Industry and Innovation 15*, 5(2008): 569–578.

Stanberry, Kurt. "The Changing World of International Protection of Intellectual Property," *Publishing Research Quarterly* 7(Spring 1991): 61–78.

Steinberg, S.H. *Five Hundred Years of Printing*, New York: Penguin, 1974.

Stiglitz, Joseph. E. *Globalization and its Discontents*. New York: W.W. Norton, 2002.

Stern, Madeleine B. *Books and Book People in 19th Century America*. New York: R.R. Bowker, 1978.

Strainchamps, Ethel. *Rooms With No View: A Woman's Guide to the Man's World of Publishing*. New York: Harper & Row, 1974.

Strong, William S. *The Copyright Book: A Practical Guide*, 5th ed. Cambridge, MA: M. I. T. Press, 2014.

Strothman, Wendy. "On Moving from Campus to Commerce," *The Journal of Scholarly Publishing 18*, 3(April 1987): 157–162.

Suber, P. (2008). *Gratis and Libre Open Access*. Web resource: Scholarly Publishing and Academic Resources Coalition (SPARC); http://sparcopen.org/our-work/gratis-and-libre-open-access./

Suber, P. (2012). *Open Access* . MIT Press; https://mitpress.mit.edu/books/open-access.

Sudhir, K. "Structural Analysis of Competitive Pricing in the Presence of a Strategic Retailer," *Marketing Science* 20(Summer 2001): 244–264.

Sugano, Joel Yutaka and Toshio Kobayashi. "Amazon.com E Commerce Platform: Leveraging Competitiveness Through the Virtual Value Chain," *Osaka Economic Papers* 52, 2 (2002): 228–258.

Sutcliffe, Peter. *The Oxford University Press: An Informal History*, London: Oxford University Press, 1978.

Sutherland, Zena and May Hill Arbuthnot. *Children and Books*. Glenview, IL: Scott, Foresman & Co., 1977.

Swain, H. "Zero Hours in Universities: 'You Never Know If It'll Be Enough to Survive;'" www.theguardian.com/education/2013/sep/16/zero-hours-contracts-at-universities.

Szenberg, Michael and Eric Youngkoo Lee. 1995. "The Structure of the American Book Publishing Industry," *Journal of Cultural Economics 18*(4): 313–322.

Taylor, Helen. *Why Women Read Fiction: The Stories of Our Lives*. Oxford: Oxford University Press, 2019.

Tebbel, John. *A History of Book Publishing in the United States, Vol. I, The Creation of an Industry 1630–1865*. New York: R.R. Bowker, 1972.

Tebbel, John. *A History of Book Publishing in the United States, Vol. 2, The Expansion of an Industry 1865–1919*. New York: R.R. Bowker, 1975.

Tebbel, John. *A History of Book Publishing in the United States, Vol. 3, The Golden Age between Two Wars, 1920–1940*. New York: R.R. Bowker, 1978.

Tebbel, John. *A History of Book Publishing in the United States, Vol. 4, The Great Change, 1940–1980*. New York: R.R. Bowker, 1981.

Tebbel, John. *Between Covers: The Rise and Transformation of Book Publishing in America.* New York: Oxford University Press, 1987.

Tellis, Gerald J. and Fred S. Zufryden. "Tackling the Retailer Decision Maze: Which Brands to Discount, How Much, When, and Why?" *Marketing Science 14*, 3(1995): 271–299.

Thomas, Louis A. "Incumbent Firms' Response to Entry: Price, Advertising, and New Product Introduction." *International Journal of Industrial Organization 17*(1999): 527–555.

Thornton, Patricia H. "Institutional Logics and the Historical Contingency of Power in Organizations: Executive Succession in the Higher Education Publishing Industry," *The American Journal of Sociology 105,* 3(November 1999): 801–843.

Thornton, Patricia H. "Personal Versus Market Logics of Control: A Historically Contingent Theory of the Risk of Acquisition," *Organization Science 72,* 3(May-June 2001): 294–311.

Tombs, Robert. "Why Design is Important: Five Designers Speak to Non-Designers," *Journal of Scholarly Publishing 33,* 1(October 2001): 37–46.

Tomkins, Jane. *West of Everything: The Inner Life of Westerns.* New York: Oxford University Press, 1992.

Thor, Andreas and Lutz Bornmann. "The Calculation of the Single Publication h-Index and Related Performance Measures," *Online Information Review 35,* 2(2011): 291–300.

Tubadji, Annie, Brian J. Osoba, and Peter Nijkamp. "Culture-Based Development in the U.S.A.: Culture As A factor for Economic Welfare and Social Well-being At A County Level;" https://doi.org/10.1007/s/10824-014-9232-3.

Underhill, Paco. *Why We Buy: The Science of Shopping.* New York: Simon & Schuster, 1999.

U.S. Department of Commerce, Bureau of the Census. *The Statistical Abstract of the United States 1980.* Washington, D.C.: Bureau of the Census, 1980.

U.S. Department of Commerce, Bureau of the Census. *The Statistical Abstract of the United States 1981.* Washington, D.C.: Bureau of the Census, 1981.

Van der Ploeg, Frederick. "Beyond the Dogma of the Fixed Book Price Agreement," *Journal of Cultural Economics 28,* 1(2004): 1–20.

Varian, Hal. "Buying, Sharing, and Renting Information Goods," *The Journal of Industrial Economics 48,* 4(December 2000): 473–488.

Waters, Lindsay. *Enemies of Promise: Publishing, Perishing and the Eclipse of Scholarship.* Chicago, IL: University of Chicago Press, 2004.

Weiss, Michael J. *The Clustering of America.* New York: Harper & Row, 1988a.

Weiss, Michael J. "The Clustering of America: Target Marketing to Book Buyers," *Publishers Weekly (*November 11, 1988b): 23–27.

Weldman, Jeffrey. "Many Are Culled But Few Are Chosen: Janson's History of Art, Its Reception, Emulators, Legacy, and Current Demise," *Journal of Scholarly Publishing 38,* 2(January 2007): 85–107.

West, James L.W. III. *American Authors and the Literary Marketplace Since 1900.* Philadelphia: University of Pennsylvania Press, 1988.

West, J.D., J. Jacquet, M.M. King, et al. "The Role of Gender in Scholarly Authorship;" https://doi.org/10.1371/journal.pone.0066212.

Weybright, Victor. *The Making of a Publisher: A Life in the 20th Century Book Revolution.* New York: Reynal, 1967.

Whiteside, Thomas. *The Blockbuster Complex: Conglomerates, Show Business, and Book Publishing,* Middletown, CT: Wesleyan University Press, 1982.

Williams, B. *Philosophy as a Humanistic Discipline.* Princeton, NJ: Princeton University Press. 2008.

Williams, Peter; Iain Stevenson, David Nicholas, Anthony Watkinson, Anthony, and Ian Rowlands. "The Role and Future of the Monograph in Arts and Humanities Research," *Aslib Proceedings 61,* 1(2009): 1.

Willinsky, John. "As Open Access is Public Access, Can Journals Help Policymakers Read Research?" *Canadian Journal of Communication 29,* 3 (2004): 381–401.

Willinsky, John, Sally Murray, Claire Kendall, and Anita Palepu. "Doing Medical Journals Differently: Open Medicine, Open Access, and Academic Freedom," *Canadian Journal of Communication 32,* 3 (2007):595–612.

Willinsky, John. "Open Journal Systems: An Example of Open Source Software for Journal Management and Publishing," *Library Hi Tech 23,* 4 (2005): 504–519.

Willinsky, John. "The Stratified Economics of Open Access," *Economic Analysis and Policy 39,* 1(2009):53–70.

Wolpert, Samuel and Joyce F. Wolpert. *Economics of Information.* New York: Van Nostrand Reinhold, 1986.

Xia, Jingfeng. "A Longitudinal Study of Scholars Attitudes and Behaviors Toward Open-Access Journal Publishing," *Journal of the American Society for Information Science and Technology 61,* 3 (2010): 615.

Vassiliou, M., Rowley, J. "Progressing the Definition of 'E-Book,'" *Library Hi Tech 26,* 3(2008): 355

Zboray, Ronald J. *A Fictive People: Antebellum Economic Development and the American Reading Public.* Oxford: Oxford University Press, 1992.

Zinkhan, George M. "The Role of Books and Book Reviews in the Knowledge Dissemination Process "*Journal of Marketing* 59(January 1995): 106–108.

INDEX

SPRINGER NATURE

GPSR Compliance

The European Union's (EU) General Product Safety Regulation (GPSR) is a set of rules that requires consumer products to be safe and our obligations to ensure this.

If you have any concerns about our products, you can contact us on ProductSafety@springernature.com

In case Publisher is established outside the EU, the EU authorized representative is:

Springer Nature Customer Service Center GmbH
Europaplatz 3
69115 Heidelberg, Germany

The manufacturer's authorised representative in the EU is Springer
Nature Customer Service Centre GmbH, Europaplatz 3, 69115 Heidelberg,
Germany. If you have any concerns regarding our products, please
contact ProductSafety@springernature.com

Printed and bound by CPI Group (UK) Ltd, Croydon, CR0 4YY
27/04/2026
02097607-0002